RUSSIA
IN
WAR AND PEACE

RUSSIA
IN
WAR AND PEACE
Alan Palmer

The Macmillan Company
New York, New York

Endpapers A soirée at Anna Scherer's; illustration to *War and Peace*

Previous page, left The buildings of Moscow often fell victim to fire in the dry summer months; but the conflagration of 1812, aided by arson and the deliberate removal of fire-fighting apparatus by the fleeing Russian authorities, surpassed any disaster the city had previously known.

Previous page, right The arms of Paul I from the Mikhailovsky palace, where Tsar Paul was murdered in 1801.

THE MACMILLAN COMPANY
866 Third Avenue, New York, N.Y. 10022

Designed by Rodney Josey
Maps by Claus Henning
Picture research by Pat Hodgson

Library of Congress Catalog Card Number: 72–89539

First Printing

Filmset by Keyspools Ltd., Golborne, Lancashire
Printed in Great Britain

Contents

MAPS AND DIAGRAMS

Author's Notes

All date references are given according to the Gregorian Calendar common to western Europe and the Americas and not, unless otherwise stated, according to the Julian Calendar which Russia continued to use until the Revolution. In the nineteenth century the Julian Calendar was twelve days behind the Gregorian Calendar. Any references to chapters in *War and Peace* are based upon the divisions in the definitive English translation by Louise and Aylmer Maude.

I am indebted to the books listed in the brief bibliographical note and to the staffs of the London Library and the Bodleian Library, Oxford, for their help and co-operation; and I am also particularly grateful to my wife, Veronica, for her assistance and her valuable comments on my manuscript.

Preface

In 1863 Leo Tolstoy began writing *War and Peace*, a book which was later described by John Galsworthy as 'the greatest novel ever written': Virginia Woolf judged its author to be 'the greatest of all novelists' on the strength of this work alone, and there are few people who would cavil at the choice of such superlatives. For the powerful moral vision through which Tolstoy chronicles the period of Russia's confrontation with Napoleon has entered profoundly into our understanding both of Western history and of human society.

War and Peace chronicles the fortunes of two families – the Rostovs and Bolkonskys – who, with their friends and dependants, are lifted by Fate out of their ordinary lives and enveloped in one of the epic tragedies of human folly, the grandeur and misery of Napoleon's final struggle to consolidate his supremacy in Europe. Other authors have sought to combine purely domestic and genuinely historical themes, and there are many who are, like Tolstoy, so sensitive to nature that their pens capture more than the outward eye perceives: but there is no-one who can rival Tolstoy in the power to describe, at once, with equal scope and facility, the confused arrogance of war, raging over a vast continent, as well as the most intimate experiences of individual human lives. He weaves the stir of a sleigh ride or the timeless majesty of an oak set among birches into a complex counterpoint with the horror of men disfigured by death, beside the icy lakes of Austerlitz or at that 'most terrible' of battles, Borodino. It is these gifts of startlingly evocative narrative which make *War and Peace* a work of such unique stature.

The novel has had universal appeal, but it is important to remember that it was written in the first place by a Russian for his countrymen. Pierre, Prince Andrew and Natasha – the principal characters in the book – act out their roles against the rich backcloth of their country's past. Behind them loom the half-Asiatic traditions of Muscovy, the mysteries of the Orthodox Church, the splendours of St Petersburg, and a social structure based on the mutual obligations and frustrations of serfdom. Historic figures – Tsar Alexander,

Prince Bagration, Marshal Kutuzov – take their rightful parts in the drama, but we see only a portion of their lives, vivid episodes in an epic and no more.

Tolstoy was describing a period in time, 'the smell and sound of which can be apprehended by us and are dear to us', as he himself wrote in 1864. More than a century later, it is difficult for those of us with a different cultural background to catch that 'smell and sound'. This present book attempts to place the events of these momentous years from 1805 to 1814 in their historical context, providing not a commentary on Tolstoy's masterpiece but an introductory survey of the Russia in which he set his greatest work. If this book in any way stimulates an interest in the age of Napoleon and Alexander, its author will be well satisfied, for he believes there are few epochs so rewarding to any reader with a feeling for the past and a sensitivity to human drama.

Elected a Fellow

OF THE HORTICULTURAL SOCIETY of LONDON

Alexander

15th June 1824

1 The Heritage of Muscovy

The signature of Alexander I on a decorative plate painted by Mrs Withers (1824) to mark the 150th anniversary of the Horticultural Society, of which Alexander was a newly-elected fellow.

ON A FEBRUARY AFTERNOON in the year 1698 curious bystanders along the banks of the Thames watched royal oarsmen conveying a foreign prince up river to Blackfriars. Although the young giant seated awkwardly beneath a canopy in King William's barge was officially incognito, everyone knew he was in fact ruler of 'all the lands of Muscovy': Tsar Peter I, whom later generations were to respect as 'Peter the Great' had come across to England from Holland as head of a mission which, he hoped, might secure political allies against his Turkish enemies and, at the same time, enable him to learn something of the manufacturing techniques of the West. He claimed that he had set out from Russia on a voyage of personal discovery: 'I am among the pupils,' he declared with heavily false modesty, 'and I seek those who can teach me.' For some four months he stayed in London, living first in Norfolk Street and later at Sayes Court, the Deptford home of John Evelyn, the diarist. Peter was a source of awed astonishment to all who encountered him, whether lumbering around the dockyards in labourer's dress, conspicuous by his great height and huge hands, or passing the night wenching and carousing with his Russian companions. Their habits were, indeed, alarming: they wrecked Evelyn's furniture and gardens, using the canvases on his wall for drunken target practice and amusing themselves boisterously with a wheelbarrow in the shrubbery. Peter's way of life was so boorish that no men of distinction in London took his political designs seriously: he was greeted with cold civility by William III and ignored by most of his ministers. Nobody believed Russia was potentially one of the great European Powers. Grudgingly, however, it was acknowledged that Peter had a gift for assimilating technical information and that he showed a shrewd ability for enlisting the help of experts, who agreed to journey to Russia and impart their skills to his backward subjects. His behaviour was so remarkable that he remained a legendary figure long after he had left for Vienna and Moscow; and it was inevitable that, in common memory, Peter should personify the distant empire of which he was master. Russia, it was thought, was a mysterious land, in Europe but of Asia; and its people seemed little better than barbarians.

One hundred and sixteen years later another Russian tsar, whom the genealogical tables showed as Peter's great-great grandson, visited London. The contrast between the two occasions provide significant commentary on the change in Russia's status. Alexander I landed at Dover on 6 June 1814, and on the following day travelled up through Kent to stay at the Pulteney Hotel, off Piccadilly. No foreign prince has ever received so rapturous a welcome from the English people. Even before it was officially confirmed that he was coming to England, there had been a brisk trade in biographical pamphlets lauding his virtues as 'a Christian Conqueror'; and for three weeks he was hailed as a new Messiah from the East, the monarch who had purged Europe from the sins of Jacobinism. His coach was cheered whenever it drove through the streets of the capital, and the daily press, which in those days was not always well-disposed towards crowned heads, recorded his progress with reverence.

The people were saluting not only the Tsar but the victories of the Russian army, which had marched from beyond Moscow to the gates of Paris in an eighteen-month campaign. The epic events of the years 1812–14 had been regularly reported, sometimes faithfully but often with exaggeration, in the daily and weekly newspapers. Everyone, it seemed, now admired the stern resolve of the Russians who had thus turned disastrous defeat into total victory, surviving the rigours of fighting through two of the bitterest winters anyone in western Europe could remember. Romance, distorting historical truth, created an idea of Russia which was at least as fanciful as the prejudiced contempt of earlier generations. The imagination thrilled to tales of sacrifice and privation; and the cheers rang out through the London streets for the Russian liberator, for his generals, and for the Cossack horsemen who had brought to their encampment in Hyde Park some of the mystery of Asia.

It is true that the Tsar's public and private remarks failed to attain the sublime level of his reputation; they were, indeed, so lacking in courtesy or good sense that they appalled both the Tories in government and the Whigs in opposition; and the Prince Regent personally thought even less of Alexander than King William III had thought of Tsar Peter. But such friction at the top was not allowed to cast shadows across the displays of popular adulation; and the Tsar was fêted wherever he went in southern England.

This mood soon passed. It was succeeded by inflated alarm at a 'Russian bogey' which was said to be menacing all the liberties of Europe. Yet the strange spectacle of 1814 and all the excitements of 'the year of revelry' were never entirely forgotten. Even in the days of disillusionment, there remained those to whom the Russian State

Tsar Alexander of Russia greeted by the Billingsgate market women in a caricature of his visit to England after the defeat of Napoleon.

was not so much a dangerous colossus as a sphinx, no less enigmatic and intriguing than in Peter the Great's time. For them and their successors, half a century later, Count Leo Tolstoy's *War and Peace* provided, if not a reading of the Russian riddle, at least a clue to its understanding; and so it has been to other generations throughout the world for more than a hundred years.

The Russia in which Tolstoy set the greatest of his novels was politically an integral part of the European system. But this was a comparatively recent development. Until the eighteenth century the evolution of the Russian State had been totally distinct from other communities farther west. The Russian lands lacked natural frontiers to the east or to the west and, in consequence, their boundaries have shifted over the centuries in a way unknown in western Europe; and so, too, has the siting of the successive centres of Russian civilisation.

The first known inhabitants of the present-day border regions of Russia were nomadic peoples who had spread westwards from central Asia and found little good land in the dark forests. During the ninth century after Christ they began to establish themselves in a chain of towns which stretched along the rivers between the Baltic and the Black Sea. In the north they set up a fortified position, which was protected by marshes, at Novgorod in the year 862. Soon afterwards another band founded a second town, a hundred miles to the west, at Pskov. Further south, almost on the watershed between the

14

РАСКОЛЬНИКЪ ГОВОРИТЪ
СЛУШШІ ЦЫРЮЛЬЩИКЪ
Я БОРОДЫ СТРИЧЬ НЕ
ХОЧѸ ВОТЪ ГЛЕДИ Я НА
ТЕБЯ СКОРО КАРАѸЛЪ ЗАКРІЧѸ

ЦЫРЮЛЬНИКЪ ХО
ЧЕТЪ РАСКОЛЬНИКУ
БОРОДУ СТРИЧЬ•

Opposite Cossacks of the Don basin. These primitive but superlative horsemen on their unlikely-looking, remarkably swift horses, were the legendary pride of the Russian cavalry.

Above The reign of Peter I saw a prolonged drive on the part of that determined monarch to crush the power of the boyars and force Russia to accept Western ideas and styles. This contemporary woodcut shows Peter the Great carrying out his edicts — the shortening of the boyars' traditional long beards.

Baltic and the Black Sea, a third town was established in 882 at Smolensk. But the principal area of settlement was well clear both of the forest zone and of the marshes: it was in the rich steppe country of the middle Dnieper, later to become the great granary of the Ukraine. At some time in the eighth century a group of hills on the right bank of the Dnieper was fortified by a band of Slavonic warriors, who named their entrenchment 'Kiev', after their chieftain; and at the end of the ninth century Kiev became the chief town in a loosely knit principality which extended up the Dnieper to Smolensk and then northwards down the Dvina to Pskov and Novgorod. From this primitive river-principality may be traced the origins of the Russian Empire.

Kiev grew rapidly into one of the main trading centres of early medieval Europe: furs and timbers came down the rivers from the north; and there was already a surplus of grain from the surrounding steppe-land. But the most important link ran along the lower waters of the Dnieper and across the Black Sea to Constantinople, capital of the Byzantine Empire. Several of the early Kievan Russian rulers, all of them warlike pagans, launched unsuccessful campaigns against Constantinople; but the ablest of them, Vladimir (who reigned from about 978 to 1015, and who was later canonised), declared his willingness to become a Christian, and he was baptised into the Greek Orthodox Church in the year 998. Although Vladimir was as bloodthirsty and ruthless as his heathen predecessors and appears to have embraced the new religion as an act of state, his conversion was an event of major importance for Russia. Christianity had been known in Kiev as a sophisticated belief of the greater families for almost half a century before Vladimir was baptised: but the conversion of the Prince led to a swift revolution in the social pattern. Orders were given for wholesale baptisms and, as Vladimir's subjects found it wise to obey their lord, Christianity spread rapidly along the rivers of Russia. With the earliest priests there came not only a beautiful form of liturgical worship but a written language, an artistic culture, and the first attempts at consistent administration and recorded government. Soon new contacts were established with the West; Vladimir's grand-daughter, Anna, even married one of the Capetian kings of France, Henry I; and foreign travellers returned home marvelling at the wealth of the Kievan cathedrals and monasteries. Less than a hundred and fifty years after Vladimir's conversion, it was said that the city of Kiev itself contained over four hundred churches, twice as many as in twelfth-century London, and though this claim may well be exaggerated, there is no doubt that Kiev attained a remarkable level of civilisation. Even in Alexander I's reign, educated Russians still thought of Kiev as a city of particular spiritual significance, 'the Jerusalem of Russia'.

But Kiev was far more vulnerable to attack than Novgorod or any of the other early town settlements. From the fourth century after

The carved ikonostasis of the gate-top of the Trinity, Kiev-Percherskaya Monastery. Kiev was called 'the Jerusalem of Russia'.

Christ onwards, successive waves of Asiatic invaders crossed the southern Russian steppes in their drive to the West. The last and greatest of these migrations, the Mongol-Tartar movement of Ghenghis Khan in the thirteenth century, found Kievan Russia easy to invade and politically too divided by factious quarrels to offer united resistance. The city of Kiev itself was sacked and burnt by the Tartars in 1240. Soon all southern Russia – and much of central Asia and Siberia, too – was brought under the suzerainty of the Tartar Khanate of the Golden Horde, a Moslem warrior empire with its centre of power on the lower Volga. For two centuries the Khanate levied tributes in money and military contingents from the Russians, but the Khans were not religious fanatics, and the Orthodox Church was permitted to safeguard its own traditions. The Mongol-Tartar conquest inevitably cut Russian links with Europe and turned the Russian people towards Asia. Eastern customs and artistic forms left their mark on the Russian way of life.

With the destruction of Kievan Russia, the towns of the north acquired new importance. Novgorod succeeded Kiev as a trading community, although the political administration of the Russian lands – such as it was – became centred on the city of Vladimir, about a hundred miles east of Moscow. The Princes of Vladimir were able to retain some cohesive unity by accepting a nominal vassalage to the Golden Horde, while protecting themselves against the incursions of Swedes, Germans and Lithuanians from the north-west. The most famous of these Princes of Vladimir was Alexander, to whom the eponym Nevsky was accorded after his great defeat of the Swedes on the river Neva in the same year as the Tartars sacked Kiev. Subsequently, at Lake Peipus near Pskov, he gained an equally famous victory over the Teutonic Knights, a military order of crusaders despatched by the Emperor Frederick II to bring the benefits of German colonisation and the Catholic religion to the eastern marchlands of Europe. Alexander Nevsky's victories ensured him a permanent place in Russian legend, whether Tsarist or Soviet, as the supreme patriot hero of the people. He was a warrior saint, a father-figure whose reputation outshone his achievement, invoked in hours of peril by Peter the Great, by Alexander I and indeed by Joseph Stalin. When Alexander Nevsky died in November 1263 he was deeply mourned: 'The sun of Russia has set,' declared the chief dignitary of the Church in Vladimir. But in reality, for Russia, it was as yet still dawn.

The half-century after Alexander Nevsky's death was marked by internal feuds over the succession within the princely dynasty and eventually by the rise in importance of the town of Moscow, where there were no privileged families or powerful merchants to curb the ruler's authority. Ivan I, who became prince of Moscow in 1325, was entrusted by the Tartars with the collection of tribute from the other territorial rulers of central Russia, and in 1328 he was permitted to

Above The landscape of Kievan Russia was dominated by majestic churches like the magnificent, eleventh-century Cathedral of St Sophia in Kïev.
Below A twelfth-century fragment of the Sigtunskiye Gate in the St Sophia Cathedral in Novgorod.

call himself 'Grand Prince of Moscow and of All Russia'. No one pretended that his policy was heroic – his contemporaries nicknamed him 'Ivan Kalita' ('Old Moneybags') – but his prudence ensured recognition of the primacy of his family by the Tartars at a time when the Khanate itself was being weakened by disputes over the succession. In 1380 Prince Dmitri Donskoi successfully defied Tartar attempts to levy new tributes and defeated the Khan's armies at the battle of Kulikovo. Although the Tartar menace remained potentially dangerous for Moscow, the Grand Principality was by now virtually independent; but it was not until the second half of the fifteenth century that the Russians found, in Ivan III, a truly national sovereign.

Ivan the Great, as he is generally known, was on the throne of Moscow for over forty years, from 1462 to 1505. His reign has a threefold significance: territorial, constitutional, ecclesiastical. At first it seemed as if he would be content to continue the expansionist policy of his immediate predecessors: by skilful diplomacy, backed by armed strength, he trebled the size of his dominions by absorbing the small principality of Tver and the much larger territories of Novgorod, lands stretching eastwards from Lake Peipus to the Ural Mountains and northwards from the middle Volga to the Arctic wastes. But he sought a greater royal dignity than any other prince had enjoyed, partly in order to achieve recognition by his brother sovereigns and partly so as to strengthen the power of the monarchy within the State at the expense of the nobility: hence, in 1498, he was proclaimed as an Emperor, 'Tsar-Autocrat chosen by God'. Yet this was not enough. Ivan finally identified his imperial authority with the mission of Orthodox Christianity. Only nine years before his accession the city of Constantinople had fallen into Turkish hands. The effects of this event were felt all over Europe. Yet while in the West a great exodus of scholars from Byzantium gave vigour to the renaissance of classical studies, the legacy of the Eastern Empire to Russia was almost entirely ecclesiastical. The Muscovite State inherited the task of preserving the Orthodox Church, a duty symbolised by Ivan's marriage to the niece of the last Byzantine Emperor. In the sixteenth century, with the Tartars of the Crimea accepting vassalage to the Turks, it did not seem as if Russia would ever become sufficiently powerful in the Black Sea to challenge the new Moslem masters of the Bosphorus. But, in later years, when the Tartar power declined, and Russia looked towards the warm seas of the south, the claim of the tsars to be heirs of the Byzantine Emperors proved a formative influence on Russia's external policy. What might otherwise have seemed blatant territorial greed was ennobled by a cloak of crusading idealism.

There were increasing contacts between Russia and the West at the end of the fifteenth century; and these links grew closer still in the following sixty years. Ivan the Great's wife, Sophia, had fled from

The first map of Moscow, drawn by Baron Sigismund von Herberstein (1486–1566) who visited Russia in 1517 and 1526.

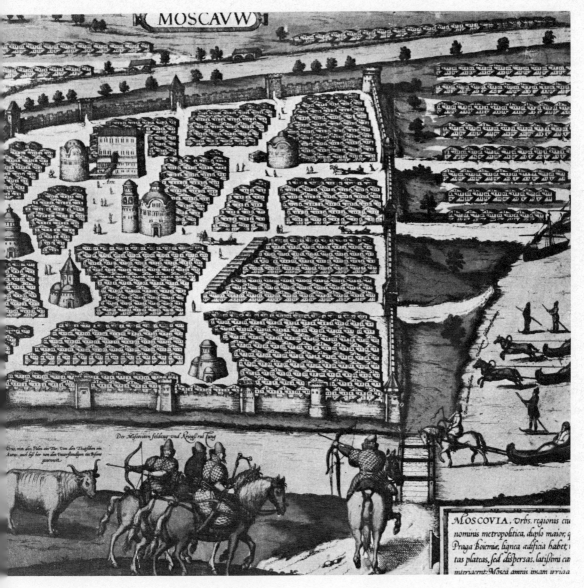

Byzantium to Rome and subsequently brought with her to Russia the first of the numerous Italian architects whose skills, blended with native tradition and craftsmanship, produced a distinctive Moscow style of building. Shortly after Ivan's death, the first diplomatic envoys from Venice and from the Habsburg Emperor arrived in Moscow. And there was a traffic the other way: Russian vessels traded with Denmark and Holland; and in 1524 one enterprising Russian aristocrat crossed the North Sea and visited London, the earliest personal link between Muscovite Russia and England. Thirty years later, Richard Chancellor made his famous journey by the northern sea route to Archangel and thence overland to the court of Ivan IV in Moscow. Since the Poles, Lithuanians and

21

Swedes were in a state of chronic warfare with the Muscovites, Chancellor's voyage had a special significance for Tsar Ivan. If Russia was cut off from western Europe in the Baltic, there was now at least a possibility of maintaining some communication by the long route around the North Cape; and Ivan sent a personal emissary back to Elizabeth I in London in 1556.

At one moment in the 1560s Ivan IV seriously considered leaving Russia and seeking sanctuary in England from Elizabeth I. He was faced by a problem which any Tudor monarch would readily have understood: a challenge to royal authority from a rebellious nobility (in Russia, the *boyar* class). Rather than go into exile, Ivan IV chose to rule by terror. He protected himself against conspiracies, real or imaginary, by recruiting a personal bodyguard, the *Oprichniki*, a police force of some six thousand men, upstarts raised from nothing by the Tsar and bound to him by the promise of land. They were permitted to use every instrument of torture and intimidation, and their cruelty became legendary. Ivan himself was suspicious, vindictive and sadistic: he killed his eldest son in a fit of anger; and on one occasion ordered his guards to seize a French envoy who had annoyed him and to nail the Frenchman's hat to his head. When he believed the people of Novgorod were in communication with his foreign enemies, Ivan sent the *Oprichniki* to ravage the city. He broke the power of the old *boyars* and made the authority of the Tsar feared throughout his lands, but at a frightful cost. His grandfather was remembered as Ivan the Great: he himself has come down in history as Ivan the Terrible. And yet, in his earlier years, he was one of Russia's most successful warrior princes, a statesman and general worthy of respect, who conquered Kazan and Astrakhan, carrying his writ to the shores of the Caspian Sea.

Western travellers who risked the uncertain temper of life under Ivan IV wrote of what they saw as though Muscovy were an extension of Asia; and in a sense they were right. Despite the influence of the Orthodox Church, the Court they visited had more in common with the Khanate than with Byzantium: and, though Ivan made much of his connections with the West, his people seemed always to look towards the East. Adventurous hunters, Cossack pioneers, traders and peasants had begun to pass through the low wooded hills of the Urals into Siberia, where there were few inhabitants and a rolling ocean of steppe-land inviting settlers to penetrate even farther into Asia. Within twenty years of Ivan's death towns were being established east of the Urals and there were primitive settlements on the Yenisei, the great river which bisects Siberia from the White Sea to Mongolia. Less than half a century later the first trading posts were established on the Pacific coast (1649). It is curious to reflect that at this particular moment the Russians were still denied access to the Black Sea, by the Turks and Tartars, and had no foothold on the Baltic, for their one narrow corridor to the Gulf of Finland had

been lost in a war with Poland and Sweden in 1617. But, in Asia,
what mattered to the Russians was not as yet the sea-coast, but the
interior of the continent and in particular the forest trails with their
promise of furs. Contact was established in the second quarter of the
seventeenth century with the Manchu rulers of China; and in 1638
the first tea chests arrived in Moscow, an almost casual introduction
of what, within two generations, had become accepted as the
national drink of all the Russian people.

The Asian influence on Muscovy was indirectly intensified by the
conflicts between the earliest Tsars and the united Polish-Lithuanian
kingdom to the west of their lands. Poland-Lithuania was the largest
kingdom in Europe for much of the seventeenth century, and whenever there were troubles over the Russian succession the Poles took
advantage of the anarchy to the east of them and pushed forward
their frontier, even occupying the city of Moscow itself from 1610 to
1612. In one sense the Polish-Lithuanian State was better placed to
become the leader of a Russian-Slavonic Empire than Muscovy:
territorially Lithuania (first united with Poland in 1385) was the
successor of Kievan Russia, controlling the whole of the later
Ukraine, except for its coastal strip; and the Poles and Lithuanians
had kept free from connections with the Tartars and their Asian

customs. Poland-Lithuania failed to retain its primacy over the eastern European isthmus for three main reasons: internal feuds at least as serious as those which weakened the Muscovite Crown; external rivalry in the Baltic with the Swedish kingdom; and, above all, because the ruling class became so closely associated with the Counter Reformation Church and with central European institutions that it could not assimilate the peculiarly Muscovite traditions nor counter the genuinely Russian feeling of religious patriotism fostered by the Orthodox Church. By the middle of the seventeenth century the Polish rulers were forced on to the defensive along the disputed Russo-Polish borderlands, and in 1667 the Truce of Andrusevo formally ceded to the Tsar the two principal historic cities of the region, Kiev and Smolensk. Most of the Ukraine, which had been in revolt against the Poles for some twenty years, was incorporated in the Russian lands at the same time.

The Andrusevo Settlement had an even greater significance. For the first time Russia gained a common frontier in the Balkans with Turkey, thus beginning a rivalry which was to endure as long as the two empires themselves survived. Turkey was a loosely knit political unit established under the Ottoman dynasty in the fifteenth century and still, in 1667, stretching from the Persian Gulf to the Adriatic Sea and from the Crimea to the Yemen. Because the Ottoman Turkish Sultans seemed weak and inefficient, successive Russian rulers were tempted to expand southwards along the shores of the Black Sea, hoping that they might eventually become masters of Constantinople and restore the Orthodox faith in the silent heart of Byzantium. But the decaying Turkish giant showed remarkable resilience. Expansion along the Black Sea was to prove a harder task for Russia than expansion along the Baltic coast.

The acquisition of Kiev and Smolensk marked the high point in the reign of Tsar Alexis Romanov, who had ascended the throne in 1645 at the age of sixteen. Alexis was a strange man, pious and austere in his earlier years, given to fits of terrifying anger and sudden moods of contrite repentance. At home his genuine desire to improve conditions was hampered by conspiracies and revolts; and, despite the apparent success of his conflict with Poland, he failed to gain land where he most needed it, in the north along the Baltic. Yet the happenings of his reign set the pattern for the following century, when Russia became accepted as a European Power. It was Alexis who first encouraged English and German agricultural experts to come to Russia, although few outside the Tsar's immediate circle took notice of their advice; and similarly it was Alexis who first took care to draft careful instructions to his envoys abroad, so as to counter the impression in foreign Courts that the Russians were a backward and barbarian people. He even opened a theatre within the Kremlin at Moscow; and he extended the practice of inviting foreign military instructors, notably from Scotland and from Prussia,

Seventeenth-century foreign ambassadors present their letters of credit in the Tsar's audience chamber.

to train his armies in the tactics of the Western countries. Tsar Alexis died in January 1676, when he was still some months short of his forty-seventh birthday: he left a son, by his second wife, a sturdy boy of three, who eventually came to the throne as Peter I in 1682 and made his famous visit to Holland and England sixteen years later. Peter the Great was to thrust Russia westwards in a way which his father, Alexis, had never thought possible – and of which he would certainly not have approved, had he foreseen its consequences.

Peter the Great created the Tsarist Russian Empire, changing Muscovy out of all recognition. Although it was in his reign that the Russians concluded their first formal written treaty with China (1689) and conducted their first serious military campaign against Persia (1722–3), Peter showed little interest in Asian questions. His fundamental purpose was devastatingly simple: he wished to make Russia a modern European State; and to this objective he subordinated both foreign affairs and his plans for internal reform. Like most great statesmen Peter was an opportunist in tactics,

25

trimming and modifying policy according to the need of the moment;
but he was also essentially a revolutionary and his work was propelled
by ruthless fanaticism, often made horrible by the streak of cruelty
in his character. He drove himself and his empire too hard and too
recklessly: few of his subjects could leap forward in history beside
him. Inevitably his policy tended to create a privileged upper section
of society which was totally different in education and mental atti-
tudes from the rest of the population. These distinctions were artifi-
cially emphasised during the later years of the eighteenth century by
further Westernisation on the part of the court and the aristocracy;
and when Russia became a belligerent in the Napoleonic Wars it
seemed to outside observers (wrongly, as it turned out) that such a
division must weaken the will of the nation to resist.

The needs of the army and the urgency of establishing a sound
defensive position for the State dominated much of Peter the Great's
policy. For more than half of his reign he was at war, sometimes with
Sweden, sometimes with Turkey, sometimes with both. His first
military venture, an assault on the Turkish fortress of Azov in the
spring of 1695, ended in failure; but by the following summer he
had supervised the construction of a naval flotilla on the river Don,
and with this new weapon he successfully besieged Azov until it

surrendered. Similarly, on a larger scale, his conflict with King Charles XII of Sweden began with a crushing defeat at Narva in 1700 which was redeemed by a decisive victory at Poltava in 1709, when Charles was forced to flee to Turkey and his Ukrainian ally was routed. Peter the Great's victories came, not merely from his sense of military command, but from the care of his planning: he was willing to encourage Augustus II of Poland to fight Charles of Sweden, knowing that both countries were essentially Russia's rivals in the Baltic and that Russia could only benefit by watching them weaken each other while conserving her own strength. For to Peter it was essential that Russia should have a port on the Gulf of Finland and a navy capable of safeguarding Russian ships in the Baltic. At Peter's accession his country's only seaport was Archangel, which was on the White Sea and ice-bound for half the year. Peter's victory over the Swedes in 1702 at Schlüsselburg (or as the Swedes call it, Nöteborg) gave Russia control of the isthmus between Lake Ladoga and the Gulf of Finland, and it was there, at the mouth of the Neva, in the spring of the year which followed Schlüsselburg, that Peter began to build the city which was to be both 'a window looking into Europe' and a capital free from the time-encrusted, half-Asiatic traditions of Moscow.

Peter the Great left his successors a standing army organised in regiments, a navy, an embryonic civil service, a nominated senate of advisers, and a synod to administer the Russian Orthodox Church as though it were a department of State. All these achievements were of major significance, even if less dramatic than his attempts to make the Russians rid themselves of the cumbersome long clothes from the past and shave off their beards. But the foundation of St Petersburg on its marshes and nineteen islands was the decisive break with the Byzantine tradition of old Moscow. Foreign diplomats always

Above The Russians led by Peter the Great (on horseback) defeat the Swedes at Poltava (Ukraine) in 1709. This was one of the most significant battles of Peter's reign, establishing the Russians on the Baltic: Painted by A. Kotsebu.

Left The medal issued by Peter the Great to commemorate the capture of Nöteborg in 1702.

thought the city unhealthy and there were Russians who insisted that St Petersburg was 'unfit for human habitation' (and not without reason, for sentries were killed on guard-duty by a pack of wolves in the centre of Russia's new capital in 1714). Yet to Peter what mattered was its position: at the head of the Baltic in the same sense that Constantinople was at the head of the Mediterranean; and so well protected by its lakes and marshes that it has never once fallen to an invading army, not even to the sophisticated weapons of Hitler's *Wehrmacht*.

By the time of Peter's death (1725) the Russians held the whole of the southern coast of the Gulf of Finland and most of the Gulf of Riga while, to the immediate north of St Petersburg, they had absorbed the coastal lands as far as Vyborg and the present-day Soviet-Finnish frontier. These acquisitions made Russia a key piece in the struggle for mastery in northern Europe, and throughout the eighteenth century Russian foreign policy responded to the changing balance

of power on the continent. Generally the Russians tended to co-operate with the rulers of Austria, who were natural allies against the Poles and Prussians, and indeed against the Turks. Although there was no outstanding dispute with France, the Russians were more frequently opposed to French support of the minor powers in Europe than associated with their designs. Towards Britain Russian policy varied, especially in the later years of the century when the British began to distrust Russian ambitions around the shores of the Black Sea and, to a lesser extent, in central Asia. But until the Napoleonic Wars the British were good customers of Russia and, in a sense, the fleets of Anson, Rodney and Hood sailed to victory on Russian exports, for the Baltic trade in timber, flax, hemp and tar was vital for maintaining the Royal Navy throughout the eighteenth century. British commerce in return ensured impoverished Russian governments and ambitious landowners of payment in gold specie, thereby encouraging growth of the luxurious way of life which the

Catherine II with sceptre and orb in the Uspensky Cathedral in Moscow, where the coronation ceremonies of the Tsars took place: Engraving by A. Kalashnikov.

Russian nobility enjoyed during these years. In 1734 a commercial treaty between Britain and Russia emphasised the close economic relationship of the two countries; and it is appropriate that foreign travellers landing at St Petersburg should have disembarked at what was known, from the first days of the city, as the *Angliskaya Naberejne* (English Quay).

Culturally, except for a few landscape gardens, the English left little mark on Russian life in the eighteenth century, although from Peter the Great's reign onwards many Scots settled in Russia, most of them as doctors, some as officers in the army and navy, and at least one (Charles Cameron) as a Court architect. The principal Western influence in literature and the arts was French, chiefly because of the primacy of Parisian culture in Europe at this time. In the second half of the century any Russian family with social pretensions tended to read and speak French as a second language. To have a French tutor in the family circle was a recognised status symbol; and it was expected that all members of the aristocracy would wear fashionable clothes of Parisian cut. Since so much of the French intellectual ferment was concerned with ideas of 'enlightenment', many features of the age of reason could be found in late eighteenth-century Russia, often existing incongruously side by side with an almost superstitious reverence for old traditions. The most effective agent of the Enlightenment in St Petersburg was the Empress Catherine the Great (who reigned from 1762 to 1796). Catherine corresponded with Voltaire, Montesquieu and Melchior Grimm, the friend of Rousseau. She encouraged the theatre, satirical criticism, academic science, vaccination and progressive educational theories; but she genuinely believed in the divine right of Tsardom, and she even made a pious pilgrimage to the holy relics of St Dmitri in Rostov. And there were others at her Court who affected rationalist philosophy and a sensualist way of life while retaining deep respect for the customs of the Orthodox faith.

Catherine herself was not a Russian by birth. She came from Stettin on the German Baltic coast and had been brought up as a Lutheran. She married Peter the Great's ineffectual grandson, who reigned briefly as Peter III in 1762. He was himself more German-Danish than Russian, for, though his mother was a daughter of the great Tsar, his father was a Duke of Holstein-Gottorp. Both Peter III and Catherine (his first cousin on his father's side, as well as his wife) outwardly accepted Russian traditions and were baptised into the Russian Church when they left their German homes for St Petersburg. Every male member of the dynasty married a German princess in the last seventy years of the eighteenth century; and although each of these brides formally abandoned her old ways on becoming a Russian Grand Duchess, the Germanic influence at Court was considerable. It was extended still farther by similar marriages on the part of the Russian aristocracy, by the large number of Germans holding positions of responsibility in the Russian army, and by the descendants of other German families who had settled in the Baltic provinces annexed by Peter the Great. These so-called 'Baltic Germans' made great contributions to Russian government and technological development: three-quarters of the members of Catherine the Great's Academy of Science had names of German rather than Russian origin; and many diplomats were recruited from this class. The loyalty of these Baltic Germans was narrowly dynastic – they were conscious of serving a ruling family more German than Russian in blood – and they often retained their Lutheran faith. At times of intensive Russian national feeling, they were objects of suspicion and hostility; and so, for that matter, were the French tutors, cooks and men of fashion who were happily patronised in more peaceful moments.

Perhaps because she was especially conscious of her German origin, Catherine the Great was a proudly Russian nationalist. She convinced herself in later years that the people who had adopted her as their ruler were happier than the western Europeans and potentially superior in intellect and understanding to nations given over to revolution. Catherine deliberately set out to emphasise the continuity between her policy of expansion and modernisation and the legacy of Peter I to Russia. Her soldiers – and, in particular, her notorious favourite, Prince Potemkin – completed Peter's task of establishing Russia as a Black Sea Power. The Crimea and all the coastal littoral from the mouth of the river Don to the mouth of the Dniester were incorporated in the Russian Empire; and Catherine was so certain Russia's future lay in the south that she insisted on having her second grandson baptised 'Constantine', so that he might be crowned as ruler of a new Byzantium when the Russians finally drove the Turks from Constantinople.

Catherine was equally determined to safeguard Russia's position in the north. By the late eighteenth century the old Polish kingdom had been torn apart by the irresponsible rivalry of feudal magnates. In 1772, 1793 and 1795 the Polish lands were partitioned by agreement between Poland's three neighbours, Austria, Prussia and Russia. Although the ancient Polish capital of Cracow went to the Austrians and the city of Warsaw to the Prussians, the largest share of the Polish and former Lithuanian territories was incorporated in the Russian Empire. The Russian frontier in the west was advanced as far as the line of the river Niemen, nearly three hundred miles farther into Europe than the boundaries of the Muscovite State at Peter the Great's accession. Among the towns acquired by the Russians during the partitions was the old Lithuanian capital of Vilna, the third most populated city in the Russian Empire at the time of Catherine's death. But, though the gains made by Russia looked impressive on the map, they were condemned as acts of cynical territorial greed by liberal writers everywhere in Europe and

One of the principal objectives of Russian policy under Catherine II was expansion towards the Black Sea, and a series of campaigns which this entailed continued until the eve of Napoleon's invasion in 1812. This engraving commemorates a Russian victory over the Turks in 1770.

America; and the Partitions belatedly stimulated an intensive Polish national pride which was to confound the political calculations of the Great Powers over the following quarter of a century, and beyond. In Poland Catherine's policy left a heritage of bitter hatred which, in retrospect, mars the splendour of her triumphs in southern Russia and on the shores of the Black Sea.

Russia was no longer 'a poor relation' of the European Powers, patronised by the West. A clear sign of the Empire's growing importance in world affairs was shown in 1780, when Catherine took the initiative in inducing Sweden, Denmark and Prussia to join a Russian-sponsored Declaration of Armed Neutrality, which challenged British rights to interfere with non-belligerent shipping during the struggle with the American colonies. What was decided in St Petersburg in the final quarter of the eighteenth century influenced the course of events as far away as the Italian peninsula, the German Rhineland, even the Americas. In the last years of her reign no sovereign was more ready to denounce Jacobinism and the evils of the French Revolution than the enlightened autocrat of All the Russias. She made Russia, for good or ill, part of the European system.

Catherine's closing days were troubled by uncertainty over the succession. In September 1754, eight years before coming to the throne, she had given birth to a son, Paul. Officially his father was Tsar Peter III and the boy was therefore a great-grandson of the founder of St Petersburg: but Catherine herself indicated that Paul was in reality the son of Prince Serge Saltykov, since Peter III was impotent. Doubts over his paternity produced strange psychological effects on Paul in later life: he deliberately moulded his habits and interests on those of Peter III, while at the same time emphasising his admiration for his ancestor, Peter the Great. Catherine herself neglected the boy, who was frequently humiliated by the favourites she collected around her; and before he was twenty he had convinced himself that his mother was planning to have him murdered, lest he become the centre of disaffection for nobles whom she had failed to reward. As Catherine had consorted with the assassins of her own husband, it is not surprising that he was uneasy.

While Catherine does not seem to have planned Paul's death, she had every intention of keeping him out of the governing circle. He was encouraged to make long journeys abroad and when, in December 1777, he became the father of a boy (Alexander) the Empress appropriated her grandson, offering him the affection and encouragement she had always denied Paul himself. In 1783 the Empress gave Paul and his wife, Maria Feodorovna, an estate at Gatchina, some twenty-eight miles from the capital. Paul settled at Gatchina, running the estate as a miniature kingdom of his own, with private regiments and a navy (on the lake) and the rigid atmosphere of a Prussian military encampment, for he admired everything connected with Frederick the Great, even drilling his men according to old Prussian manuals of instruction. Towards the end of her reign Catherine resolved to pass over Paul's rights and proclaim Alexander as her successor. Such an act would have been fully in accord with Russian practice, for Peter the Great had abolished primogeniture as a principle of succession in 1722, declaring that the autocrat of the day had the right to decide to whom the crown should pass upon his death. But Catherine's plan came to nothing: Alexander only gave his consent very reluctantly, in a letter to the Empress written six weeks before she died; and his hesitancy, together with her own procrastination, left everything undecided. Paul hurried to St Petersburg as soon as he heard of his mother's collapse, and was proclaimed 'Emperor and Sole Autocrat of All the Russias' on 7 November 1796.

In later years people remembered Paul as 'the mad Tsar'. He sought to enforce trivial decrees banning 'revolutionary' waistcoats and determining the shape of hat that was to be worn in the streets; and he showed a macabre delight in having Peter III re-buried alongside Catherine II. More alarming were his fits of ungovernable rage. Although some aspects of his administrative policy were

A family portrait, painted by R. M. Lisiewska in 1756, of Catherine the Great, her husband, Peter III, and their son, Paul I. This family relationship was highly suspect and the common belief, fostered by Catherine, that Peter III had been impotent and was not Paul's father, created in Paul a neurotic determination to prove himself of legitimate birth.

basically sound, the nobility resented his attacks on their displays of
ostentatious living, and he rapidly made enemies among the landowning class. Moreover it was unwise of him to diminish the
privileges of the Guards Regiments while elevating the sycophants
who had served in his Gatchina battalions. He also rewarded his
friends with gifts of state lands, thus handing over some half a million
serfs to the custody and caprice of masters who had already shown
total insensitivity to the men in their care at Gatchina. The new
Tsar's foibles and eccentricities alarmed foreign diplomats in St
Petersburg and made his own sons fear for their lives, as he had
himself under Catherine.

No one could be certain from one month to the next what Paul's
foreign policy would be. For eighteen months he emphasised his

Grand Duke Paul of
Russia with his wife
Maria Feodorovna:
Watercolour by
H. Löschenkohl.

desire for peace, distinguishing himself only by revealing to the Austrians a state secret entrusted to him by his friend, King Frederick William II of Prussia. In the autumn of 1798 he went to war with France over a matter of absurd unconcern to Tsardom: on Bonaparte's occupation of Malta, Paul was offered and accepted the Grand Mastership of the Order of the Knights of Malta, a religious relic of medieval chivalry subject to the Pope's authority (and, incidentally, expecting celibacy from its members). It is difficult to see how a tsar could reconcile patronage of the Order with his obligations as champion of the Orthodox Church; but Paul took his duties as Grand-Master extremely seriously and requested the French to surrender the islands they had seized. Not unnaturally, the French ignored Paul's representations. The Tsar thereupon made a treaty of alliance with Russia's most persistent enemy, Turkey, and sent a Russian squadron through the Bosphorus and Dardanelles to assist Turkish vessels in attacking French ships and outposts in the eastern Mediterranean; and in the following year he despatched a Russian army to join the Austrians in marching against the French satellite republics in northern Italy. This expedition was commanded by Marshal Suvorov, the most distinguished Russian soldier of the eighteenth century, and it was at first highly successful. But Paul came to resent Suvorov's popularity and alleged that the Austrians were repeatedly insulting the Russian flag. After six months of joint operations Paul sent a message to the Emperor of Austria informing him that he was withdrawing his men. When, in the following year, the British expelled the French from Malta, the Tsar insisted that the British occupation of the island was an affront to his dignity and gave orders for 20,000 Cossacks to march from their garrison town of Orenburg (Chkalov) to invade British India, nearly two thousand miles away. Like most of Paul's projects, this plan bore no relation to reality. The expedition set out across the Central Asian wastes but made little progress, and many of the Cossacks perished from the hardships of a journey undertaken with no proper system of victualling or supplies.

By the autumn of 1800 the mood of the Russian capital was sombre. Paul's eldest son, Alexander, had already sent a letter to his former tutor in which he declared: 'My unhappy country is in a state of chaos which cannot be described' and added that it was 'a toy in a madman's hands'. Now Paul's second son, Constantine, was even more outspoken: 'My father has declared war on common sense, firmly resolving never to conclude a truce with it.' Inevitably, despite stringent security, conspiracies began to be hatched: it was impossible to leave so much power in the hands of an autocrat whose mind was so twisted. Paul, of course, suspected treason and shut himself up in a new fortress, the Mikhailovsky Castle, with grey stone walls like the Bastille, a moat like the Tower of London, and five drawbridges normally manned by units from the old Gatchina battalions. To overthrow Paul would be a difficult task at any time; and no conspiracy could possibly succeed without the approval of the heir to the throne, Alexander, and the co-operation of the Governor-General of St Petersburg, Count Pahlen.

Tsar Paul trusted Pahlen, who was efficient and had no personal grievance against his sovereign. But Pahlen was extremely cool and calculating. Secretly he convinced Alexander of the need to force Paul's abdication and the young Grand Duke offered his support provided that Pahlen gave an oath assuring him that his father's life would not be in danger. On 23 March 1801 Pahlen's conspirators, supported by the Semeonovsky Guards Regiment (in which Alexander held command), seized the Mikhailovsky Castle in the early hours of the morning and prepared to depose Paul. In the confusion a group of the plotters, who had drunk heavily, attacked Paul as he stood beside his bed and one of them throttled him by pressing a malachite paperweight against his windpipe. It was announced that the Tsar had died from apoplexy; and the capital warmly hailed the accession of Alexander 1, a handsome young giant of twenty-three.

Alexander, the Tsar of *War and Peace*, is one of the greatest rulers in Russian history: he is also the most enigmatic. In later years Napoleon remarked: 'It would be difficult to show more intelligence than the Emperor Alexander; but I find there is something missing in him; and I have never managed to discover what it is'. He possessed charm, he was willing to agree with anyone rather than provoke an argument, and once away from the parade-ground he was modest. And yet he won a reputation for insincerity and dissimulation. He was an idealist too cautious to act on the 'noble sentiments' which people applauded in his public and private utterances; and sometimes he deceived even himself. To some observers it seemed as if he were trying to reconcile two contrasting personalities at war with each other in his mind, just as in his youth he had sought to make himself agreeable to both his grandmother and his father. It is not, however, the whole picture. Behind all his actions remained doubt, uncertainty and a sense of guilt; for Alexander could never rid his memory of his father's fate. Although he had asked for a pledge safeguarding Paul's life, did he really suppose that his father could surrender the sacrosanct titles bestowed on him in all the solemnity of a coronation? No Russian emperor had voluntarily laid aside a crown placed on his head with the blessing of the Church. It is hard to see how the conspirators could carry through their design without killing the Tsar. And for the rest of Alexander's days the shadow of the sin of parricide continued to trouble him. As an act of redemption, he was compelled to lead Russia to the military triumphs which seemed unattainable so long as the Empire was under his father's uncertain direction; but as an act of contrition he felt bound to turn increasingly to religion and the consolation of the scriptures. Hence

Baron Gerard's portrait of Alexander 1.

there are moments in his reign when he seems to retreat from the reality of power politics into a haze of mysticism. Alexander was by no means a conventional warrior emperor.

Soon after his accession the young Tsar made it clear that he wished to rectify many of the personal injustices of Paul's reign and to introduce measures of reform at home. Until the closing months of 1811 attempts were made to modernise the Empire's government and legal system, notably by Alexander's close friend, Michael Speransky (1772–1839); but domestic politics were increasingly overshadowed by the great events beyond the frontiers. For these were years of upheaval in Europe, when the triumphs of French arms wrought more changes in a decade than the continent had known for many centuries. The genius of Napoleon Bonaparte – First Consul from the close of 1799 to the spring of 1804 and thereafter 'Emperor of the French' – carried France to victory over all her neighbours on land and introduced a rational pattern of administration in regions as far apart as the north German plain and the

Opposite Empress Elisabeth Alexeevna (1778–1826) wife of Alexander I. She married Alexander in October 1793 and her loyalty to him persisted despite his infatuation with a Polish countess, who bore him two children.

Left M. M. Speransky (1772–1839) the statesman largely responsible for Alexander's measures of home reform.

foothills of the Apennines. It was impossible for any ruler of Russia to ignore the Napoleonic Revolution.

When Alexander came to the throne he already had a clear concept of international policy: 'If I make use of arms . . . it will only be to repulse an unjust aggressor, to protect my peoples or other victims of an ambition which is alarming for the safety of Europe,' he declared in July 1801. He regarded Russia as a satiated power, in terms of territory and people within Europe: expansion was justified only at the expense of Turkey. To some extent he was prepared to isolate himself, in those early years, from the great contest in Europe so as to concentrate on the improvement of administrative government within his Empire. But for him isolation was based on an assumption of strength. He believed that Russia's size and military reputation entitled her, as of right, to serve Europe as an impartial arbiter. Although he had a natural fear of revolutionary Jacobinism, he had no quarrel with the France of the Consulate. Indeed, since he believed the First Consul was offering both enlightened reform and the respect of a stable political order, the Tsar had some sympathy with Napoleon's objectives.

From 1801 to 1804 Napoleon believed he was treating Alexander personally with respect and consideration. Friendship with a neutral Russia had attractions for France: it provided a means of putting pressure on Austria and Prussia; and it deprived the British of a commercial customer, perhaps even of an ally. Alexander was accordingly invited by Napoleon to assist him in 'mediating' over the future of the German princes, and his father-in-law in Baden was tactfully promoted to the dignity of an Electoral Margrave. But reality for Alexander fell short of expectation. 'Joint mediation' meant to Napoleon a simple formula of action – France decided, Russia approved. Such offhand treatment offended the Tsar. And other affronts, too, began to rankle. There was trouble over Italy, Alexander claimed a protective right over the King of Sardinia-Piedmont, an old ally of Russia; and there was also trouble over Hanover, which the French occupied without thinking to consult Alexander first (and, indeed, there was no reason why they should have done). Russian suggestions that Malta might be placed under Alexander's protection were received coolly in London and with distinct hostility in Paris. Finally, in September 1803, Napoleon publicly insulted the Russian ambassador, whom he accused of conspiring with his enemies within France; and the Tsar became convinced the French would never accord his Empire the status to which it was entitled. On 14 March 1804 the Duke of Enghien was abducted from Baden and subsequently shot at Vincennes: the Tsar saw this tragic episode as a double insult, offending the sanctity of royal blood and violating the territory of a prince with whom he had such close connections. It only needed the formal assumption by Napoleon of the title of Emperor in the following May to confirm

Illustration for *War and
Peace* of a soirée
held in the Salon of
Anna Scherer.

Alexander's growing belief that action must be taken in order to contain the renewed ambitions of the French.

Tolstoy begins *War and Peace* at a soirée held in the salon of a cultured aristocrat, Anna Scherer, at St Petersburg in July 1805. Her guests discuss, partly in Russian and partly in fashionable French, the prospects of war with Napoleon, or as they prefer to call him 'Buonaparte', for they maliciously enjoy emphasising his non-French origin. To them he is not a true Emperor of the French but the 'Antichrist', responsible for the kidnapping and execution of a Bourbon Prince (the Duke of Enghien) and, more recently, for extending the power of his own family through the establishment of satellite principalities in the Italian peninsula. For most of these members of the nobility, Tsar Alexander's policy of hostility to Napoleon therefore possesses much of the character of a crusade, endowed with a lofty idealism.

It is a superb opening scene which at once throws the reader into the political uncertainties of the moment – the tiresome prevarication of Austrian diplomacy, the conflict of war-party and peace-party in neutral Prussia, the deep-rooted suspicion of 'England's commercial spirit'. The atmosphere of tension is conveyed with scrupulous accuracy, even to the extent of showing how absurd were many of the ill-formed judgements of the time: Russia did, indeed, await the coming of war in 1805 with eager expectancy and shattering over-confidence.

2 Holy Russia

RUSSIA AT THE DAWN of the nineteenth century was an empire of slightly more than forty-one million people. Yet the country was so vast that many travellers hastening along roads across endless plains or through forests of conifers thought considerable tracts of land totally uninhabited. Their accounts show how often they were amused to hear Russians speak of mere clusters of simple homes as though they were flourishing settlements: 'The Tsar's realm is no more than an empire of villages,' declared one German merchant making his way to Moscow during Paul's brief reign. This impression, like so many recorded by foreign visitors, was superficial; but it contained an element of truth. Catherine II, in 1775, formally declared that two hundred and fifty villages were henceforth to enjoy the status of cities; and other towns came into being no less casually, growing slowly into urban communities. In 1777, when Alexander I was born, three Russians in every hundred lived in a town: at his accession in 1801 it was nearly seven. These figures show how conditions were changing; but in Prussia almost a quarter of the population were town-dwellers by the end of the Napoleonic Wars; and in England and Wales more than a third of the people lived in urban concentrations, old or new.

While western Europe was already beginning to become industrialised, economic life in Russia remained primitive. There was no active native-born capitalist class of any significance, nor could there be any genuine proletariat so long as the economy rested on obligations of personal serfdom. Most people lived and worked on large self-contained estates. Their homes were either hovels around a church, or a group of one-storey huts in a forest clearing. Towns were primarily commercial markets set at trading crossroads. Often they had developed on the site of old fortresses. Many of them were still protected by ramparts, formidable obstacles even in 1812, as Napoleon found at Smolensk. Distances were so vast in Russia and communications so bad that it was rare for anyone to have personal knowledge of a town not in the immediate vicinity of his home,

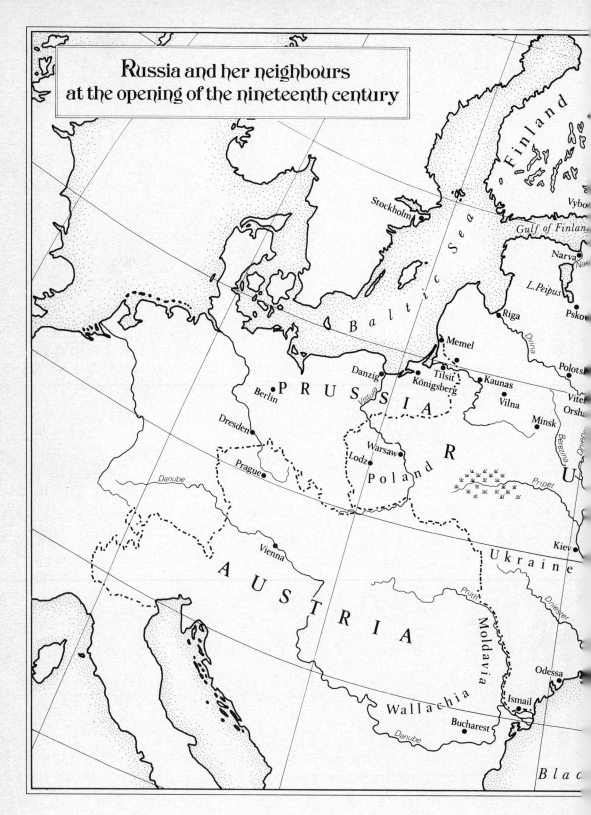

Russia and her neighbours at the opening of the nineteenth century

Finland

Stockholm

Baltic Sea

Gulf of Finland

Vybo

Narva · Nar

L. Peipus

Riga

Psko

Dvina

Memel

Polots

Danzig · · Tilsit

Berlin · **P R U S S I A** Königsberg · Kaunas

Vilna

Vite

Orsha

Dresden · Minsk

Vistula

Berezina

Warsaw

Lodz

Dnie

Prague · **P o l a n d** **R** Pripet **U**

Danube

Vienna Kiev

U k r a i n e

A U S T R I A Pruth

Dniester

Moldavia

Odessa

Ismail

W a l l a c h i a

Bucharest

Danube

B l a c

500 km

Archangel

Lake Ladoga

Neva

St.Petersburg

atchina

Novgorod

S i b e r i a

U

r

a

l

Perm

Tver

Volga

Yaroslavl

Vladimir

Nijni-Novgorod

Kazan

Mozhaisk

MOSCOW

Vyazma

Moskva

Oka

Kaluga

Simbirsk

Smolensk

Tula

Orel

S

S

I

A

Orenburg

Ural

Voronezh

Kharkhov

Poltava

Don

Dnieper

Volga

Ekaterinoslav

Alexandrovsk

Taganrog

Astrakhan

Caspian Sea

Sea of Asov

rimea

Caucasus

Sebastopol

Sea

unless he was a member of the governing classes or had marched with the army on one of its European campaigns. When, at the end of the Napoleonic wars, the Russians began to roll westwards across Germany, it is probable that not more than one man in ten had any real acquaintance with town life. For them, as for other invaders before and after, soldiery was to prove a remarkable instrument of social education, disconcerting in its implications both for the conquerors and the conquered.

On the eve of the French Revolution monarchy was still recognised as the natural system of government by almost every community in Europe and Asia. Despite the egalitarian sentiments of American colonists and enlightened men of letters in the West, hereditary right to personal allegiance was believed to ensure continuity, stability and social cohesion, whether in the Britain of George III, the Prussia of Frederick II, or the Persia of Karim Khan; but the nature of monarchical institutions varied considerably from country to country. Most continental rulers followed the French pattern, established by Louis XIV and providing a pretentious façade for administration from above. Yet there were two monarchies on the fringe of Europe whose systems were distinctive, though at opposite extremes from each other: in Britain the Crown remained the centre of political life even if all effective power was curbed by parliamentary restraint; and, by contrast, in Russia the authority of the sovereign was subject to so few limits that there was virtually no political life at all, but only a contest between courtiers eager to attract the attention of a monarch whose sanction was necessary for every act of policy or administration. In western Europe the idea of a king as patriarch, the 'breathing image of God', was no longer fashionable at the end of the eighteenth century: in Russia, on the other hand, the ruler continued to enjoy 'all the reverence due to a divinity', as an English envoy reported to London soon after arriving at St Petersburg in 1777. There were simple homes in Russian towns and villages where candles burnt before portraits of Peter the Great long after his death, even though in his lifetime he was an enemy of the more superstitious forms of religious devotion. The Tsar's authority had been proclaimed sacrosanct by monastic writers early in the sixteenth century and, although the outward form of his rule was modified in Peter's reign, nothing was allowed to lessen the holy aura of the sovereign in full state. Catherine II may have been a Protestant convert and a usurper with no claim to the Russian throne, but by her coronation in Moscow she became the Chosen One of the Almighty. 'The Lord has placed the Crown on thine head', declared the principal bishop of the Church: woe to the sinner who defied the elect of God.

The power of the Tsars was not subject to constitutional restraints nor to the exercise of customary rights by ancient cities or other corporations, as was so often the case in western Europe. Theoretically the monarch was responsible only to Almighty God for his

The Virgin of Smolensk at the Novodevichy Monastery in Moscow, covered in gold and precious stones contributed by the sixteenth-century Tsar Fedor (son of Ivan the Terrible) and his wife Irina. The crown of real jewels was probably added by Fedor's daughter Sofya (sister of Peter the Great) who died in exile at the monastery.

actions. He could appoint anyone he wished to a military command or to serve as a minister of State; he might decide the amount of direct and indirect taxation without conceding rights of representation to any class among his subjects; he could establish committees of ministers to examine legislation or review policy, but he was not obliged to accept their recommendations; and he determined the general pattern of foreign relations, adjusting them as he chose, even to the extent of abandoning an ally in favour of agreement with a former enemy. Administrative officials, high and low, wielded authority only so long as they retained the monarch's confidence. Some of them had considerable powers, notably the governor-generals of St Petersburg and Moscow, who in the sovereign's absence were virtually viceroys with the right to regulate the life of their city by proclamation and decree; but there was no hereditary post whose holders might challenge the imperial authority. Peter the Great had established a Senate in 1711 which, for more than two centuries, served as the ultimate judicial and administrative body in the Empire: but the Tsar nominated every Senator, and the responsibilities of the Senate were so defined and amended by successive rulers in the eighteenth and early nineteenth centuries that it could never threaten the constitutional structure of the State. Alike in peace and in war, there was no regular procedure for determining what should be done over any question: matters were settled by the ruler in council with whom he wished and meeting wherever he chose to be. In theory the Tsar might be a wise and enlightened father of his peoples or an arbitrary tyrant: but in practice he relied on the goodwill of the landed aristocracy and the support of the soldiery under arms. In the thirty-seven years between the death of Peter the Great and the accession of Catherine II, there were six rulers of Russia; and each of them depended, for retention or loss of the throne, on the military backing of the Guards Regiments which Peter had created in his standing army. By the beginning of the nineteenth century it was tacitly accepted that the military needs of the state could determine the way in which the power of the autocrat was allowed to function.

But the unique characteristic of Russian Tsardom remained the close interdependence of secular and ecclesiastical authority. Ever since Peter the Great's reforms the official Russian Orthodox Church had been essentially an extension into spiritual matters of the cumbersome bureaucracy of the Russian State. Its affairs were controlled by a Synod, headed by a lay official whom the Tsar nominated. Since the authority of the Church permeated every village, the priests were frequently treated as agents of the government and were expected to make known to their congregations all proclamations and decrees. The 'Spiritual Regulation' – a constitution for the Church issued by Peter in 1721 and based on the canon law of German Protestantism rather than the Orthodox tradition – specifically

Easter procession in seventeenth-century Moscow.

required a priest who heard of any seditious matter, even within the secrecy of the confessional, to inform the civil power so that action might be taken to safeguard the State. The bishops and priests fulfilled a double service to the existing order in the eighteenth and early nineteenth centuries: they preserved the Byzantine ideal of an emperor (*autokrator*) who owed his princely dignity to God alone and who was 'Supreme Judge' of the affairs of the Church as well as of State; and they also emphasised that what mattered for the ordinary believer was not the day-to-day problems of material existence but betterment of the soul, a condition achieved through devotional exercises which would ensure eternal salvation

for those who practised them reverently, and which at the same time would allow the devout to experience a sense of 'heaven on earth' within the mysteries of worship. This mystical feeling of inner contentment encouraged a fatalistic acceptance of suffering and of redemption through pain. Negatively it thus helped the Russian people to find strength with which to bear the burdens of an often drab existence in peace and in war. It was condemned as a creed of social conservatism by those who failed to understand the inspirational nature of the Orthodox faith.

The Russian Church always puzzled foreign visitors by its combination of hierarchic pomp and simple piety. They complained, not without reason, that the priesthood attached less importance to the moral law than to the prophets, that they strove less for observance of the commandments than of the beatitudes. Many travellers wrote scornfully of the superstitious hypocrisy they found in Russian religious observance. William Richardson, the son of a Scottish Presbyterian Minister, was in Russia from 1768 to 1772 as tutor to the family of the British Ambassador; and he was horrified by the ritual of a Church with which he could never sympathise. On one occasion, he wrote:

It is pretended that its principles are pure and rational. The practice, I am sure, is different. I may tell you of pompous ceremonies, magnificent processions, rich dresses, showy pictures, smoking censers, and solemn music; but I cannot tell you that the clergy in general are exemplary, or the laity upright. . . . Were I not an eye-witness, I could scarcely conceive it possible that men should so far impose upon their own minds, as to fancy they are rendering acceptable service to Heaven by the performance of many idle ceremonies, while they are acting inconsistently with every moral obligation.

In the 'Spiritual Regulation' Peter the Great had warned the bishops against an indolent and decadent priesthood, instructing them to see that the clergy 'walk not in a dronish lazy manner, nor lie down in the Street, nor tipple in drinking places, nor boast of the strength of their hands'. But these precepts were not always observed.

Whatever its shortcomings, the Church played a major part in every Russian's life. It created a sense of community, a feeling of 'togetherness' within a huge family of which the Tsar was 'the little Father'. While the bishops and archimandrites would parade golden ikons with rich ceremonial on every festival of State and Church so as to identify temporal and spiritual authority, the priests taught an egalitarian humility of all believers before the sacred relics of the Faith. The surging chant of unaccompanied singing, the long line of acolytes bearing candles and holy banners and the perfumed clouds of incense offered a climax of religious ecstasy for the simple and for the sophisticated alike. As a social influence the Church was as omnipresent in the Russia of Alexander I's reign as in the Roman Catholic lands of the Mediterranean.

53

Not all the drama of the Orthodox Faith was enacted in its great cathedrals. Even William Richardson was grudgingly impressed by the ceremony of blessing the waters which was celebrated in St Petersburg on the Feast of the Epiphany. He described the scene as he saw it in the early 1770s but his account could equally well apply to the opening decade of the new century, for the ritual changed little with the passing of the years:

A pavilion supported by eight pillars, under which the chief part of the ceremony was performed, was erected on the Moika, a stream which enters the Neva between the Winter Palace and the Admiralty. On the top was a gilded figure of St John: on the sides were pictures of our Saviour, represented in different situations; and within, immediately over the hole that was cut through the ice into the water, was suspended the figure of a dove. The pavilion was surrounded with a temporary fence of fir branches: and a broad lane from the palace was defended on each side in a similar manner. This passage, by which the procession advanced, was covered with red cloth. . . . No parade of priests and Levites, even in the days of Solomon and by the banks of Shiloh, could be more magnificent. After the rite was performed with the customary prayers and hymns, all who were present had the happiness of being sprinkled with the water thus consecrated and rendered holy. The standards of the army and the artillery received similar consecration; and the rite was concluded with a triple discharge of musquetry.

This account by Richardson emphasises the close association between the ceremonies of Holy Russia and the army, a link traced back over the centuries to the almost legendary feats of St Alexander Nevsky. It helps to explain the deep religious feeling which was so marked a characteristic of the Russian soldiery during the 1812 campaign and which is recorded in the memoirs of the period. Tolstoy describes how, on the eve of battle in September 1812, a guard battalion bore the sacred ikon of the Holy Virgin of Smolensk from the church of Borodino to the village of Gorki through the assembled troops, who knelt by the roadside in prayer as the procession moved forward. It was an occasion remembered not only by eye-witnesses on the Russian side, but by the enemy across the valley. General Count Philippe de Segur wrote of the incident later: 'Credulous from ignorance, they worshipped their images, fancying themselves devoted by God to the defence of Heaven and their consecrated soil.' But this scornful comment by a French rationalist merely shows how far was the invader from understanding the Russian mentality. In kneeling before the holy relic, Marshal Kutuzov (the Russian commander-in-chief) and his troops were not seeking divine assistance in the forthcoming battle, like Cromwell's Ironsides before Marston Moor: they were accepting the existence of a spiritual power more enduring than the temporal powers locked in battle and symbolised by created objects of artistic beauty present amid the ugliness of war. They knelt in reverence and in fatalistic subjection to the will of God; and it is this quality of other-worldly

The Virgin of Smolensk was one of the most revered objects of the cult of the Virgin; a similar ikon was worshipped by Kutuzov and his men at Borodino, within sight of Napoleon and his marshals.

lowliness of the person which most perplexed observers from foreign lands, whether fighting beside the Russians or against them.

It would, of course, be false to assume that all Russians shared the same religious convictions. To a far greater extent than in the armies of the West, the Russian officers and men believed in a God which was beyond human comprehension. Most of them accepted the teachings of the official 'Synodical' Orthodox Church because it was the principal educational and cultural influence on their lives, dominating the little art and music that they knew, regulating their weeks of restraint and pleasure by a calendar of fasts and festivals, and dazzling their eyes by the beauty of holiness embodied in the Liturgical pageant. But there were some sincere Christians for whom the Synodical Church was too much a projection of the State, and who, even before Peter the Great's reign, had clung to old ritual rather than accept the reforming tendencies of the seventeenth century. A schism began in the 1650s between the official Church and a group known as the *Raskolniki*, generally translated as 'Old Believers', although 'Conservative Ritualists' would give a more accurate impression of their attitude of mind. For more than two centuries these dissenters held fast to their conviction that the essence of Orthodoxy was to be found in the spiritual life of the inner man, rather than in a church that was compromising ancient tradition by new notions imported from the West and which emphasised the virtues of service to the State and to the Tsar who was its embodiment. It is difficult to assess the importance of these 'Old Believers' in the first decade of the

The initiation ceremony of a nineteenth-century Russian Masonic lodge; Count Pierre Bezuhkov undergoes this trial in Tolstoy's *War and Peace*.

nineteenth century. Numerically they were comparatively few and were mostly concentrated in colonising communities in remote regions such as the Don basin or western Siberia, but several merchant families in Moscow were *Raskolniki* by inclination. Although the Old Believers were never radical revolutionaries, like some of the Protestant dissenting sects, they tended to show many of the qualities of hard work and sobriety associated in the West with the centres of Calvinistic business enterprise.

Naturally there were intellectuals in St Petersburg who had absorbed enough of the teaching of the Enlightenment to believe that true religion consisted of respect for humanity and social justice, and there was a strong sentiment of Voltairean deism in the salons of the capital. During Catherine the Great's reign Freemasonry had spread in the twin centres of Moscow and St Petersburg although it was always more explicitly mystical than in the Lodges of Germany and the West. Freemasonry was attacked by Catherine II in the last years of her reign as a subversive doctrine, but it was tolerated again by Alexander, even though the Orthodox were

Above Jewish merchants drawn by Davidoff in 1840. The Jews were a conspicuous element of Russian society, notably in Vilna and Riga.
Right The ritual implements of masonic practice.

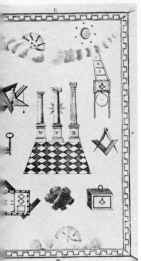

threatened with excommunication if it was known that they had taken masonic vows.

The westward expansion of Russia in the late seventeenth century brought a large Jewish community within the jurisdiction of the Tsars and of the Orthodox Church. Although anti-Semitism had never been a characteristic of the old Muscovite State, the Church leaders assumed a hostile attitude towards the Jews which was particularly marked in the last years of Catherine II and was certainly not relaxed under her grandson. A decree of December 1791 confined all Jewish believers within a Pale of Settlement which comprised the Polish lands and Lithuania, most of the Ukraine (but not the city of Kiev) and the provinces of Vitebsk, Poltava and Ekaterinoslav. The Pale was thus more than two hundred miles west of both St Petersburg and Moscow, and did not include even the western cities of Smolensk and Kharkov. The principal urban concentration was in Vilna, the third largest town in the Empire in 1812 and an accepted centre of Jewish intellectual and cultural life. Although the Jews were not so openly persecuted as in the last half-century of Tsarist rule, they remained a caste apart and no attempt was made to assimilate their traditions to the Russian way of life. They received, it should be added, little sympathy or encouragement from the Napoleonic invaders.

Although the ideal of 'Holy Russia' as an exclusively Orthodox community was dear to the hearts of the Synodical Orthodox and the Old Believers, there were adherents of other Christian faiths in Russia during Alexander I's reign. German Lutheranism kept its appeal to members of the landed aristocracy from the Baltic provinces, especially after the exodus from Germany of Prussian Junker families who could not accept collaboration with the French. There were also, particularly in southern Russia, evangelical groups of Germanic origin, mostly adherents of some form of Baptist belief. In both St Petersburg and Moscow there was a fashion among aristocratic ladies for Roman Catholicism, as Tolstoy recalls in describing the conversion of Helene Bezukhova. Although the numbers involved were few, some had considerable influence. In Moscow, for example, the wife of the Governor-General of the city, Count Rostopchin, was induced to change her faith and to worship, with other ladies of distinction, at the church of Saint-Louis-des-Français: it was, apparently, spiritually satisfying to make confessions in French rather than in the language of the common people; and Madame Rostopchin found it pleasanter to converse 'with more elegant and better-educated priests than the simple Russian pastors' (or so, at least, writes her daughter).

Finally there remained, as always in Russia, eccentric sects who rejected all organised religion, believing that the faithful might commune directly with God. These included the *Straniki* ('wanderers'), who held that holy poverty and vagrancy ennobled the spirit, and the *Dukhobors*, who favoured a communal existence with all property shared. Alexander I treated most of these dissenting sects with tolerant understanding, even though proselytism among Orthodox believers was officially contrary to Russian law. In 1805 the Tsar permitted the Dukhobors to settle in a community of their own near Melitopol, between the lower Dnieper and the Sea of Azov. He showed sympathy, too, towards isolated monastic settlements and individual hermits. This respect for 'holy men' (*starets*) ran deeply through Russian life: for the desire to withdraw from reality into a condition of religious contemplation was widespread. Tolstoy describes the appeal of the simple 'God's folk' to Princess Marya Bolkonskaya and her wish to set out on a pilgrimage:

She pictured herself . . . dressed in coarse rags, walking with a staff, a wallet on her back, along the dusty road, directing her wanderings from one saint's shrine to another, free from envy, earthly love, or desire, and reaching

at last the place where there is no more sorrow or sighing, but eternal joy and bliss.

Marya Bolkonskaya never made the pilgrimage: nor, one suspects, did many others who felt a similar longing for the simplicity of religious retreat.

Ever since the early sixteenth century devout believers had held that Moscow was a 'holy city', 'the third Rome', the heir both to an early Church betrayed by Papal aberration and to Byzantine Orthodoxy, which had been extinguished by the Turkish seizure of Constantinople in 1453. Moscow in 1812 was still the repository of the soul of Holy Russia. It was a national shrine full of priests and monks and worshippers, a city of glittering domes, pointed spires and cupolas, with a prayer-calling tintinnabulation constantly resounding through its squares and echoing from its walls. Robert Lyall, a Scottish physician who visited Moscow seven years after the French occupation and who published a 'detailed history' of the city on his return to Britain, found that even in 1819 he could count six cathedrals, twenty-one monasteries and 274 churches within the thirty square miles of the town limits; and seven years earlier the number must have been greater still. Until the fall of the Empire in 1917, the tsars came to Moscow for the solemn occasions of State. They were crowned in the Uspensky Cathedral within the courtyard of the Kremlin, a church of mixed Byzantine and Lombard style, so that ornately carved columns support a five-cupola roof. After coronation they proceeded to pray before the relics in the Archangelsky Cathedral and the Blagoveshchensky Cathedral, with its nine domes. All the churches of the city were rich in ikons and vestments, the whole atmosphere heavy with centuries of accumulated piety, dim lights gleaming mysteriously on gold mosaic and hazy silken canopies. To some visitors the Faith seemed oppressively omnipresent. Catherine II, who had accepted every act of coronation ceremonial when she was unsure of her position on the throne, later turned against the religiosity of Moscow, holding it to be a protective covering for fraud and sedition: 'Never had a people seen before its eyes more objects of devotion, miracle-working images,' she declared, 'more churches, more of the priestly band, more convents, more holy hypocrites, more beggars and more thieves.' She preferred the sophistication of St Petersburg; but her grandson, Alexander, respected the traditions of Moscow, easily identifying himself, whenever he visited the city, with its tremendous sense of a holy past; and so it was with many of his subjects.

But Moscow was not only a religious centre. Ever since its establishment the city had served a thriving merchant community. At first traders exchanged goods in the *Kitai Gorod*, a huge open area to the north-east of the Kremlin walls, which is often translated as 'Chinese City', although it is probable that the words have a partially Mongol origin and mean 'Central Fortress'. By the end of the

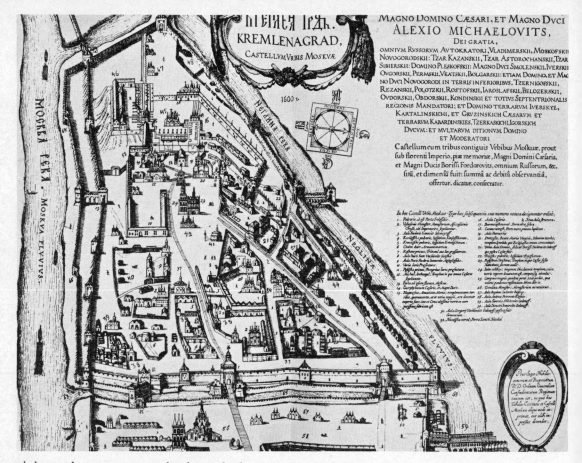

A seventeenth-century plan of the Kremlin.

eighteenth century most business deals were concluded, not in the *Kitai Gorod*, but in Ilinka Street, where tea-rooms clouded with the vapour of steaming samovars fulfilled a similar social function to the coffee-houses of the City of London in Queen Anne's reign; and Ilinka Street – which is nowadays known as Kuibyshev Street – became accepted as the financial centre of Moscow in much the same way as Lombard Street in London. Ordinary selling of goods still continued in the *Gostinnyi Dvor*, a labyrinth of shops and passages off the *Kitai Gorod* on the east side of Red Square, similar in style and function to the bazaars of Asian cities. It was there that travellers bought the silver spoons, which the Russians delighted to make, and the bracelets and snuff-boxes from Tula. Silks from the Caucasus were on sale, together with religious bric-a-brac; but there were also sections of the Bazaar where people could buy the essentials of life as in any other market, fish from the rivers, meat and vegetables; and once the frosts came, it was possible to preserve some of the rarer types of carcases in a primitive natural deep-freeze which was conveyed to Moscow for sale during the hard months of winter.

Outside the city, where in earlier reigns there had been villages and military cantonments, the first factories began to develop in the

Opposite St Basil's Cathedral in Moscow, one of the most familiar Kremlin buildings, in an unusual view which shows a river outlet in the Kremlin walls with boatmen and washerwomen at work: drawn by A. G. Vickers c. 1864.

60

Above An antiques stall in
early nineteenth-century
Moscow, displaying some
of the oriental wares
which were exchanged in
the Kitai Gorod.

Left The frozen meat
market in Moscow
attended by peasant
traders of the late
eighteenth century.

opening years of the new century. Since the Napoleonic Wars cut off Russia from the textile industry of the West, local initiative succeeded in producing woollen goods and clothing of cotton and silk. Most of the work was undertaken in small shops with only a handful of workers, but the first survey made in Moscow after the French occupation showed that there were twenty-two undertakings on the eastern outskirts of the city which employed a labour force of more than a hundred, and a cotton spinning factory (using hand-looms) with nearly six thousand workers. There was also a woollen industry, which was technically extremely backward, but which used serf labour in order to keep the army supplied with cloth for its uniforms; this, too, came from Voronezh and Simbirsk. It would, of course, be a mistake to exaggerate the extent of nascent industry: it was a portent, rather than a significant aspect of life in the city at this time.

Foreign travellers noticed more interesting sights – the long walls of the Kremlin, a citadel town in itself; the contrast between Italianate palaces and the poverty around the city gates; the variety and colour in dress of the peoples who had flocked in from the eastern lands. Catherine Wilmot, a highly intelligent Irish woman in her early thirties, came to Moscow at the end of 1805 as a guest of Princess Dashkova; and in a letter to one of her younger sisters she described the city as 'this lazy, idle, magnificent and Asiatic town' from which 'all effective power has long since passed to . . . Petersburg'. To Catherine Wilmot 'Moscow is the imperial terrestrial political Elysium of Russia'. Her Scottish contemporary, Robert Ker Porter, who visited the city for the first time a few months later, saw it differently. He was then aged twenty-nine, and already enjoyed a reputation as an artist who painted battle scenes and panoramas on a grand scale. The frivolous side of life in Moscow appealed to him, and he could not treat the city with the mystical, reverential awe which so many Russians accorded it. He found Moscow 'a world of palaces collected together. . . . It is not a city of houses in mere rank and file of streets, but rather a collection of mansions, each embosomed amidst its own lawns, gardens, pleasure grounds and the dwellings of its necessary slaves'. 'Pleasure is ever the order of the day,' he declared, so that life became 'a continual carnival where balls, private theatres, masquerades and assemblies of all sorts, forever vary the scene'. The people of Moscow surprised him by their liking for seeking pleasures out of doors, picnics in the summer and sledging parties in winter. To his sister, he wrote in the early summer of 1806:

The grounds around the mansions of the nobility afford romantic and charming morning walks. But their favourite amusement is what they call the *promenade*. It consists of all the carriages in the city, perhaps to the number of seven thousand, trailing after each other in regal procession, through fixed parts of the town and its environs. The insides of these vehicles are filled with all the beauty and splendour of Moscow: and in my life I never beheld so many lovely women at one time.

Ker Porter believed that aristocratic ladies in Moscow possessed a greater beauty than the women at Court in St Petersburg: he suggested that the difference was caused by 'the intermarriage of the noble families with those of countries celebrated for symmetry of features and graceful forms, namely Circassia, Georgia and Poland'. As he later married one of them (Princess Maria Shcherbatova), his pen may have been coloured with excessive partiality. He thought that 'the young ladies dressed in rather the Parisian mode, but much improved by their own taste'. Catherine Wilmot disagreed with him. She described how she had seen:

Wives and daughters and granddaughters beautifully dressed sitting in gilded Boudoirs with Slaves dancing before them burning perfumes and handing sweetmeats to their Visitors etc. etc. etc. But tho' the french manner is universal, the Language spoken, the dress precisely the same, the kissing every instant in Salutation, and the youngster educated by french Mademoiselles and Monsr. l'Abbes, yet they are neither well bred nor agreeable Women but obvious imitators and as such overacting the externals without having the slightest pretensions to that soothing suavity of manner which pleases so universally in France.

Both Catherine Wilmot and Ker Porter spent their evenings in the pleasures of the highest strata of society. While the serfs appear occasionally in their narratives as extras in the wings, the middle

Opposite Catherine the Great in the uniform of the Semeonovsky Guards: contemporary portrait by Erichson (?).

Moscow's Back Yard: a painting illustrating the way that nineteenth-century Moscow was composed of costly houses and churches juxtaposed in random fashion with shacks, gardens and plots of open land.

classes hardly ever take the stage. Once Ker Porter noticed the wives of some of the merchants as he walked through the gardens which separated the Kremlin from the river, and he was not impressed. 'They are dressed in all the riches their husbands can afford, in a fashion hot, stiff and most discordant with their figures,' he wrote, 'Their complexions are besmeared with white and red paint ... not a muscle of their face ever moves ... they stand like a string of waxen figures, gazing on the passing groups of the higher orders.' It is an unkind picture: but no one, native or foreigner, seems to have felt sympathy with such blatant social climbing.

There was an artificial character about much in Moscow society during these years, and taste showed at times a vulgar exuberance. The aristocracy patronised concerts in private mansions as they did in Vienna, Dresden or any other great cultural centre of the West. Yet it was only in Moscow that one would find a princely guest ending the musical evening by carrying his host shoulder high from the room in order to prove that, though in middle age, he had not lost the muscular strength which had made him a living legend in his youth. That restless commentator, Sir John Carr (whom Byron once dubbed 'Europe's wandering star'), was horribly fascinated by the contradictions he found in the cultural life of the Moscow aristocracy. He described his impressions in a book published in 1805:

The nobility ... live in the voluptuous magnificence of eastern satraps: after dinner they frequently retire to a vast rotunda, and sip their coffee,

The rough and tumble of Russian Court life.

during a battle of dogs, wild bears and wolves; from thence they go to their
private theatres, where great dramatic skill is frequently displayed by their
slaves, who perform and who also furnish the orchestra. These people are
tutored by French players who are very liberally paid by their employers.

Although the private theatres might mount a play by Molière or
Racine the best households still retained dwarfs and fools, who would
provide a crude knockabout entertainment for the guests. 'I . . .
sometimes almost fancy myself transported back to the feudal days
of Britain,' wrote Ker Porter after some months of hospitality in an
aristocratic household. But, like most visitors, he was amazed at the
standards of French cooking in the kitchens of the Moscow nobility
and delighted by its variety. 'Green peas and asparagus are here as
common at Christmas as potatoes and winter cabbages may be with
you,' he told his sister in a letter home, and he mentioned to her how
he had been given 'fruits of every climate, ripened in hothouses, and
vegetables of all descriptions raised in cellars.'

Sometimes, according to Catherine Wilmot's sister Martha, the
dinners in Moscow would continue long into the night: 'Four hours
uninterrupted cramming of every delicacy that nature and art can
produce,' she wrote. Improbably these vast banquets were succeeded
by long sessions of vigorous dancing. The formal deportment of the

Below High society in
early nineteenth-
century Moscow
included the theatre
amongst its obligatory
pursuits. This lithograph
by Duruy captures the
sort of occasion during
which, in Tolstoy's *War
and Peace*, many
significant meetings
were made.

minuet, which had been stylized by an instruction manual at the end of Catherine II's reign, gave way to the excitement of the polonaise and later of the waltz. The delights of a Grand Ball in Moscow were always less refined than in the new capital. To some visitors they seemed extremely exhausting. 'Luxuries and magnificence soon lose their effect,' complained Catherine Wilmot in February 1806, 'and the unnatural hours kept here totally destroy every species of pleasure when once the gloss of novelty is at an end.'

Not all the entertainment in Moscow took place under directly aristocratic patronage. The city had a tradition of public dramatic performances, a feeling for theatre. In the first years of Alexander's reign, the commonalty as well as the nobility were becoming accustomed to opera, ballet and plays in the Petrovsky Theatre, which seemed so massive to the citizens of Moscow that they called it quite simply the Bolshoi (Large) Theatre. From early days it was closely associated with the Moscow Orphanage, a grandiose white stone building on the banks of the Moskva River, founded in the 1760s and providing children trained by Italian dancing masters so that they could perform in ballet or take supporting roles as mutes in opera and conventional drama. Unfortunately this first Bolshoi Theatre was destroyed by fire in September 1805 and its successor was not opened until January 1825; but during the intervening two decades Court patronage kept the theatre active with performances in one of the princely palaces and in a wooden amphitheatre along the Arbat Street. In Moscow it was accepted that the theatres, whether stone or wooden, should have a gallery for less wealthy patrons as well as the customary tiers of boxes for the nobility.

There was always a considerable risk of fire in Moscow. Many of the outer districts were crowded with wooden gimcrack homes and, although there were primitive fire appliances which were stationed at the chief vantage points within the city, the prospects of halting a severe conflagration were slight. Water was extremely scarce. Only a few wealthy homes had wells of their own. Elsewhere, whether the water was needed for drinking, washing, or fire-fighting, it had to come from the Moskva River or its small tributary, the Iauza. It was always impure and, towards the end of summer, there was an inevitable drought as the water-level fell in the two streams. The facilities for fighting any fire in August or September were few and depended to a large extent upon the initiative of a handful of watchmen, who seem to have been no more and no less efficient than Shakespeare's Dogberry and Verges. It is significant that Napoleon's entry into Moscow in mid-September 1812 should have coincided with one of the most dangerous times of the year, a long and dry summer breaking up into squalls, and a north-west wind funnelling down narrow streets and out across the great square beyond the Kremlin to lash the bazaars of the *Kitai Gorod*. Probably, even in peacetime, there would have been a serious fire that autumn, for until the

Above The Samson fountain, part of the later, baroque ornamentation to Peter the Great's palace outside St Petersburg, carried out by the architect Rastrelli.
Below The domes of the chapel on the Catherine Palace at Tsarskoe Selo near St Petersburg.

second week of September the weather had been unusually hot: but the circumstances of a foreign occupation and a virtual emptying of the city by its inhabitants made disaster inevitable. Three-quarters of the buildings in Moscow went up in smoke and flames.

Before the Great Fire of 1812 Moscow looked most impressive from four or five miles distant, gilded spires and burnished cupolas rising in coloured fantasy over the flat and open countryside, an Asian mirage beckoning to Europe. St Petersburg, too, possessed a mysteriously refractive quality, translucent under the clear northern light. Most foreign travellers approached St Petersburg by water, sailing into the shallow mouth of the Neva from Kronstadt and the Gulf of Finland, watching from the deck as forest, marsh and mudbank receded and the towers and palaces of a northern Venice stood out above the blurred melancholy of silent islands. Others saw the city first from the Oranienbaum Road, as Catherine Wilmot did,

The river Neva; an engraving by Makaev which shows the classic beauty of St Petersburg. The buildings in the foreground are the Admiralty and the Academy of Sciences.

receiving a general impression of 'Imperial residences', 'sweetly cultivated . . . lawns' and 'astonishing beauty rising up at either side'. Whichever way the visitor came, his route would eventually lead him to the great square beside the Neva where Catherine II had erected Falconet's equestrian statue of the city's founder. The memorial is rich in symbolism. Peter the Great sits astride a horse which rears itself up proudly from a massive pedestal of Finnish granite, its hoofs trampling on a coiled snake: the Tsar, who rather strangely is depicted in the traditional Russian dress he so detested, stretches out an arm towards the river and the site of his original settlement. It is by no means certain if the snake represents envy or

The statue of Peter the Great in Senate Square, St Petersburg.

obscurantism, nor whether Peter's imperious gesture shows affection, possessive pride, or defiance of the Neva's waters threatening to inundate the city. But it is at least clear which way the Tsar is pointing: in commemorative bronze, as in real life, he looks perpetually towards the Gulf and the sea-lane to the West. In Alexander's reign St Petersburg was still fulfilling the triple function of Peter's grand design: a capital city for the new Russia; a modern port remaining free from ice for seven months of the year; and the principal recipient and transmitter of European culture within the Tsar's dominions.

Inevitably the imperial responsibilities of St Petersburg overshadowed the city's other roles. Nearly half the population at Alexander's accession were either employed in the civil service (as executants or petty bureaucrats) or formed part of the garrison attached to the Court. And even more people were indirectly dependent on the city's status as a capital, for the administrative nobility had large numbers of retainers who would not have resided in St Petersburg except for their master's obligations to serve the Tsar. Government was thus, in a sense, the principal industry of the city; and it remained so throughout Alexander's reign. Moreover many of the craftsmen who worked in the capital owed their occupation entirely to the needs of the Court. Five of the comparatively few small factories established in the late eighteenth century catered solely for the luxury trades and tastes of the nobility: one made porcelain; another printed playing cards; two rivalled each other in processing macaroni; and a fifth produced elegantly designed wallpapers. A list of business enterprises in St Petersburg in 1794 shows the importance of aristocratic fashion to the commercial community: there were fourteen manufacturers of lace, seven of silk and twelve of hats. Over the following quarter century the pattern seems to have changed little. Even the earliest conventional, heavy industrial plants originally sought to meet the slightly artificial needs of an elegant capital: thus the famous iron foundry and engineering works established at the end of the eighteenth century by the Scottish entrepreneur, Charles Baird, began by concentrating on the special machinery for the endless building operations undertaken by the government; and later it was Baird's who cast the great iron dome of the Isaac Cathedral.

'What a city! Magnificent beyond description or imagination,' declared the eccentric English soldier, Sir Robert Wilson, when he made his first visit in 1807; and he added, 'It is, I am certain, unrivalled on the continent and in the modern world for the grandeur of its buildings.' Successive rulers over half a century had sought to leave their mark on the beauty of Peter's creation. The Empress Elizabeth, who had reigned from 1741 to 1762, employed an Italian architect, Bartolomeo Rastrelli, to build the Winter Palace, although it was not completed until after her death. Catherine II found that, with a mere 1500 rooms, Rastrelli's palace was too compact for her

The Grand Chapel of the Winter Palace.

needs and she commissioned the construction of three annexes to the Winter Palace: a Hermitage pavilion built by the French architect Vallin de la Mothe in 1765; the Hermitage Gallery, designed by a Russian, Yuri Velten, ten years later, in order to house her collection of old masters; and the Hermitage Theatre, added by the Italian Giacomo Quarenghi in 1780. As Catherine also authorised the building of a Marble Palace for her favourite, Gregory Orlov, and the vast Tauride Palace for her lover, Potemkin, she was responsible for embellishing St Petersburg with a spacious dignity which no other city in northern Europe possessed. Although Greco-Roman inspiration ensured a unity of form between the various palaces, each seemed to swagger with an individual flourish, more baroque than formally classical. With façades plastered and ornamented in red and yellow or blue and white, with sweeping colonnades and decorated porticoes, and with their line of balconies and shuttered windows in pale green, the palaces appeared deliberately to mock the grey northern skies with a palette of Mediterranean colours.

Not everyone shared General Wilson's enthusiasm for the city. 'I have seen the [Winter] Palace and 'tis Magnificent, boundless and comfortless,' declared Martha Wilmot, with her sound Irish good taste, soon after arriving in Russia in 1805. Robert Johnson, one of the first English tourists to come to Russia after the 1812 campaign, was disappointed with the Tsar's capital. He was deeply moved by

Above The Winter Palace; built by the Italian architect Rastrelli for the Empress Elizabeth. Begun in 1754 it was the greatest monument of Elizabeth's reign.

Opposite The dining-room of the Palace of Pavlovsk, one of the residences of Paul I built by the Scottish architect Cameron (1782–6).

74

the beauty of Moscow but he found St Petersburg incomplete and lacking in harmony: 'Everything as it were in outline, nothing perfect, nothing to please; everything to astonish; a mixture of splendid barbarism and mighty rudeness.' Although St Petersburg was a planned community of fine squares, long boulevards and ostentatious public buildings, there was a marked difference between the elegance along the Neva embankment and the cramped suburbs on Vasilevsky Island or out towards Peterhof. The city was as full of contrasts as Moscow, but since the poverty was starkly new it seemed disturbingly anomalous. Moreover beyond the southern approaches to the capital was another belt of luxurious living, the summer villas of the nobility, set in 'English' gardens with neat lawns and shrubberies. Finest of these palaces was the imperial residence at Tsarskoe Selo, intended by Catherine to serve St Petersburg as Versailles did Paris and Schönbrünn Vienna. There were times when foreign travellers began to wonder if the pursuit of pleasure had not become to the Petersburg nobility a substitute for religion, with one temple at the Tauride Palace and the other at Tsarskoe Selo.

St Petersburg was an expensive city in which to live. Necessities of life, such as food and timber, had to be purchased from a retailer at a high price compared to Moscow. Moreover the city was at a considerable distance from most noblemen's estates. There was often a significant contrast between the sumptuous salons, tastefully

decorated in damask and silk, and the private rooms to which the family retired after their daily performance in the pageant of public life. A climate in which, according to official observations, it either rained or snowed on half the days in the year wrought havoc with the fabric of homes and palaces; and it was difficult for many families of distinction to keep up the elegance which foreign visitors expected if they were forced to live in such an unsuitable corner of the Empire. With the coming of the dogdays in summer the great houses were left almost deserted, as families set out for their country estates or for the delights of Tsarskoe Selo and its satellite palaces. Some of the nobility still, of course, maintained a mansion in Moscow, although they tended to stay there only during periods of political displeasure, when the old capital offered a discreet place of exile from the new.

It would be a mistake to over-emphasise the difference between the social round of life in St Petersburg and in Moscow. Both had accepted alien habits although generally modifying them to local needs. In the late eighteenth century, for example, the idea of the

Skaters on the River Neva in the early nineteenth century.

Opposite The state bedroom of Empress Alexander's mother Empress Maria Feodorovna, at Pavlovsk, a summer residence of Tsar Paul I near St Petersburg.

'English Club' became popular, first in the northern capital and later in Moscow as well. But the Club tended to be not so much a centre for relaxed social life, as a place in which politics might be discussed freely, often in a spirit hostile to the existing administration; and as such it figures in the second part of Tolstoy's *War and Peace*, when old Count Rostov arranged a dinner at the English Club in Moscow for Prince Bagration, after the Austerlitz campaign. And there were variations, too, in commerce. St Petersburg, like most financial centres on the continent, had its Bourse (*Birzha* in Russian), but it was only in the second quarter of the nineteenth century that it began to resemble the stock exchanges of the West. Originally the *Birzha* occupied an impressive building along the banks of the Neva and it was purely a place where merchants might meet, conclude deals and exchange information: even at the end of the Napoleonic wars it was still predominantly informal in character and most of its members were foreign traders resident in St Petersburg. Government securities were offered for sale for the first time in the *Birzha* early in 1809, when the blockade and counter blockade of the rival belligerents virtually destroyed neutral Russia's Baltic trade. But throughout Alexander's reign the *Birzha* remained primarily a commodities exchange, taking its name from the stock markets of the West though absorbing few of their conventions.

In the theatre, on the other hand, it was not so easy to see the distinctions between Russia and the West, nor indeed between St Petersburg and Moscow. Foreign actors, actresses and dancers were welcomed in Russia up to the eve of Napoleon's invasion and there was particularly sympathy for the dramatic traditions of France. One of the most enlightening descriptions of the theatres in St Petersburg comes from the pen of Sir John Carr, himself an aspiring playwright, who visited Russia early in Alexander's reign. He thought some of the plays and opera he saw coarse and obscene, but he was impressed by the realistic scenery and by the Kamennyy Theatre (or Grand Imperial Opera), the principal home of opera and ballet in St Petersburg until the last years of the nineteenth century. His account of the theatre emphasises similarities and differences with the London of his time:

The front is a noble portico, supported by doric pillars; the interior is about the size of Covent Garden, of an oval shape, and splendidly but rather heavily decorated. . . . It frequently happens that servants stand behind their masters or mistresses in the boxes, during the performances, and present a curious motley appearance. . . . The curtain ascends at six o'clock precisely. No after-piece, as with us, only now and then a ballet, succeeds the opera, which is generally concluded by nine o'clock, when the company go to the Summer Gardens, drive about the city, or proceeed to card and supper parties. . . . It is not an ungratifying sight to pause at the doors and see with what uncommon skill and velocity the carriages, each drawn by four horses, drive up to the grand entrance under the portico,

The Bolshoi Opera
House, principal home
of opera and ballet in
Moscow in the nineteenth
century. Here, as also in
St Petersburg, patrons'
coachmen kept warm by
the fires of the little iron
huts during the
performance:
Engraving by Dubois
after Courvoisier.

receive their company and gallop off at full speed: pockets are very rarely
picked, and accidents seldom happen.

It is interesting to note that the atmosphere of the Kamennyy
Theatre corresponds closely to the setting of the opera house in
Moscow which Tolstoy chose for the introduction of Natasha to
Anatole Kuragin: there was, in reality, no building of comparable
grandeur at which opera was performed in Moscow at this time,
because of the destruction by fire of the first Bolshoi Theatre in 1805.
In general the theatres in St Petersburg appear to have been more
exclusively aristocratic than their counterparts in the older capital.

St Petersburg was inevitably a far more secular city than Holy
Moscow. Although occupational statistics of early nineteenth century Russia are far from scientifically reliable, it would appear that
upon Alexander's accession there were ten times as many priests,
clerical dignitaries and monks in Moscow as in St Petersburg; and
it is significant that ecclesiastical buildings had not as yet begun to
figure among the architectural sights of the Russian capital. Soon
after the city's foundation a small wooden church was erected and
dedicated to St Isaac of Dalmatia. In 1770 work began on the re-
placement of the church by a massive cathedral, a project in which
Catherine II always showed interest. But the new Isaac Cathedral
was not completed until after her death and it never became either a
dynastic or a patriotic shrine. The Romanovs themselves were in-
terred in a mausoleum within the Church of St Peter and St Paul,

Opposite Enamelled portrait of Tsar Alexander I on a gold snuff box presented to the Duke of Wellington in 1826.

the great fortress facing the Winter Palace across the Neva; and the religious centre for the new capital in the eighteenth century was the monastery of St Alexander Nevsky, the seat of the Metropolitan of Petersburg. The crack Guards Regiments had garrison churches of their own, fashionable places of worship but never regarded as retreats for religious devotion. It is almost as if the State was so conscious of its omnipotence that it kept all religious expression under strict control. But Tsar Alexander himself always particularly revered the Holy Virgin of Kazan, and in 1802 he authorised the building of a new cathedral (once again on the site of a smaller church) which was dedicated to the Virgin of Kazan and finally consecrated in 1811. With a huge cupola and cross and a quadruple colonnade of pillars, the Kazan Cathedral became the principal building project in St Petersburg during the years of tension between Russia and Napoleonic France. Prince Kutuzov knelt in prayer there before setting out for the army in the field, and it was there that Alexander sought spiritual consolation in the days following Borodino. After 1814 the Kazan Cathedral was recognised throughout the capital as a shrine of thanksgiving for victory, its arches hung with trophies of war and the tomb of Kutuzov accepted as a place of national veneration. But in earlier years St Petersburg society troubled little over its devotions, except for the festivities of Epiphany and Easter; and the battlefield of Europe seemed far away indeed.

Below Kazan Cathedral, built by Alexander I and consecrated in 1811; General Kutuzov was buried in the cathedral on the spot where he prayed before setting out to meet the French in 1812.

An idyllic watercolour by
Patersen of the
Tavrichesky Palace; the
wealthy proprietors
stroll in the parklands
where their serfs
are gardening.

3 Silent Obedience

CONTEMPORARY MEMOIRS and the vivid narratives of foreign travellers frequently drew parallels between life in Russia under Alexander I and the hidden volcano of revolution so long ignored by the aristocracy in eighteenth century France. There was, however, no real comparison between the social structure of the Russian Empire and living conditions in France or any other western European nation. In the West wealth depended upon ownership of land and wise investment, while the status of nobility sprang either from eminence of birth or from royal favour; but in Russia the prosperity of a noble was counted by the number of male serfs whom he owned, and his class status rested on a concept of direct service to the state. Since ancestry was theoretically of no account, it was possible for someone of humble origin – often a foreigner – to attain high rank in Russian society, provided he served the Tsar and did not merely accumulate money as a merchant; and it was also by no means rare for a junior member of some ancient family to sink to a subsistence level hardly distinguishable from the peasants around him.

The unique character of the Russian nobility sprang, like so much else, from the reforms of Peter the Great. Until the end of the seventeenth century the Muscovite State was frequently menaced by the power of overmighty landowners, the magnates (*boyars*) who had schemed against Ivan the Terrible and whose successors continued to plot against the sovereign for more than a hundred years. Peter declared that a man's status in society should be decided entirely according to his rank, which in its turn was to depend upon his efficiency and the degree of service he rendered to the State. In 1722 he regularised this principle by publishing a 'Table of Rank', which remained operative in the nineteenth century. The table was divided into three parallel columns, representing the hierarchical structure within the Court service, the civil service, and the military service. There were fourteen grades of rank, ranging from chancellor and field-marshal in the first grade down to collegial registrar and ensign (military) in the fourteenth. All officers became members of the

Aristocratic Diversions

Aristocratic activities in St Petersburg traditionally
included musicianship, dancing and theatricals. Many
serfs were specially trained to combine these forms of
entertainment with their duties, but their masters, too,
liked to cut an elegant figure.

Below Aristocratic
harpist; painter unknown.

Three portraits by
D. G. Levitsky
(1735–1822): *Left*
Countess Borschtchova;
Below Duchesses
Chovanskaya and
Chrustcheva dancing the
parts of Lise and Colin in
La Fille mal gardée;
Right Harpist
G. I. Alimova.

hereditary nobility and so did civil servants in the top eight grades: they, and their children, might own both land and serfs, were exempt from taxation and from corporal punishment and were excused compulsory military recruitment (if not already serving in the army or navy). The lower six civil grades enjoyed what was known as personal nobility, with privileges not extended to the family as a whole. Much of this system was borrowed from Prussia and Denmark; but Peter made it more an instrument of authoritarian government than in any other country. Elsewhere – in England, France, the Rhineland, Bohemia, Hungary – certain families were associated with particular counties or provinces; but in Russia proper there were no longer territorial associations for the noble families, although the peculiar structures of the Polish and Baltic lands added in the eighteenth century modified this particular principle which Peter had laid down.

Peter's reforms imposed more duties than rights on the nobility. They were expected not only to serve the State but also to train themselves and their children for service: male adults had to render an occasional account of the way in which they had fulfilled their obligations; and the government officially took note of the existence of aristocratic children from the age of ten upwards. So severe was Peter's system that he even required members of the nobility to submit a certificate of completed education before permitting a marriage to take place. He also sought to counter an old evil in the system of inheritance, by a decree which imposed upon the owner of the estate an obligation to leave it intact to any one of his heirs, rather than split it among his children, as was customary in Russia. This innovation was at least as unpopular as the insistence on education, and was held by a number of Orthodox theologians to run counter to divine justice since it denied children an equal share in their father's wealth.

Naturally Tsar Peter's totalitarian regimentation did not long survive its creator. Within forty years of his death the nobility had emancipated itself from most of the restraints he imposed. The law of inheritance was annulled as early as 1730, and by 1762 the whole concept of compulsory State service had been swept aside, except in time of war. Catherine II certainly believed that the nobility should render some part of their active lives to the service of the State, and in practice most of them continued to do so, partly because they wished to figure in a fitting grade on the Table of Rank and partly, one suspects, from a simple desire to enjoy themselves in St Petersburg or Moscow. In the 1770s Catherine began deliberately to encourage the nobility to leave the capital cities, improve their estates, and serve the Empire in provincial and county assemblies. This was a wise policy. Absentee landlords took little interest in scientific methods of cultivation: residence on their estates might have improved the productivity of the Russian countryside and could well have countered

The relationship of serf to master in many aristocratic households was an insidious amalgam of duty, worship, and fear: Engraving after Yvon.

the dangerous alienation of the nobleman from those who worked his land. Unfortunately most members of the nobility could see in Catherine's decrees merely a new charter of rights, confirming old privileges and exemptions while giving them even wider powers to exploit their serfs. Under the impact of Napoleonic invasion the principle of service, so recently a corollary to the nobleman's rights, began to assert itself once again; but this time it was not only the nobility and gentry who responded to the patriotic emergency, nor indeed were they as a class the most affected by its disasters.

The nobility, of course, had no direct share in the control of central government; and they did not seek it. Most landowners were content with a free hand to administer their estates as they thought fit, to exact services and payments from their serfs, and to amuse themselves according to the titular rank which they still claimed as rightfully theirs. When Paul issued decrees limiting the independence of the nobility, imposed liability to corporal punishment upon them, and sought to revert to the Petrine system of entailing estates, the nobles turned against the Tsar; they supported the conspirators who murdered him, and duly received from Alexander an assurance that he intended to respect the privileges which his grandmother had confirmed to them. On their own estates it seemed as if they would enjoy virtually unlimited power, with the prospect of further gifts of land and people to supplement the one and a third million adult males already given by successive rulers to the nobles in the preceding sixty years. The serf-owning nobility were the sovereign's representatives in the vast rural regions of Russia: they fulfilled the tasks undertaken in a more highly organised community by magistrates, by tax-collectors, even by recruiting sergeants. As late as 1840 the Tsar's police chief in St Petersburg liked to think of the landowner, somewhat idealistically, as 'the unsleeping watchdog guarding the State', dutifully vigilant in the most remote areas of European Russia, a temporal arm of the priesthood in preserving the fabric of autocracy. This picture was truer still in earlier years, when communications between the cities and distant estates remained hazardous and when the landowner's authority was curbed by only the most formal restraints. Serfs may not have been his slaves, but they were his chattels: he could sell them collectively or individually to another landowner; he could order their marriage or forbid it; he could assign them to the army or to distant colonial outposts in Siberia; he could have them imprisoned or mercilessly flogged. They, in their turn, were required by law to render 'silent obedience' to their master.

Theoretically there were plenty of guarantees defining the relationship between lord and peasant. In practice, the legislation was loosely phrased and difficult to enforce. How were the authorities to discover abuses so long as the law denied a peasant any right of complaint against a landowner? Some of the most intelligent foreign travellers

On many occasions serfs suffered dreadful brutality as well as humiliation. Demonic forms of flogging were devised to punish real or imaginary offences.

in Russia argued that conditions of serfdom could not be so black as they were painted since no one complained of what was done to them; and yet sometimes landowners took a terrible vengeance on peasants who had sought even the most moderate improvement in their way of life. Martha Wilmot, in 1807, was appalled to learn that Princess Dashkov's daughter had ordered a servant and his wife to be publicly flogged because the Princess, hearing that the servant had already been unjustly whipped, rebuked her daughter and aroused her fury. And there were other instances where travellers were shocked by the casual inhumanity meted out by their hosts to the household serfs: a whipping for one, for spilling the salt; a birching for another, for having allowed himself to be suspected (wrongly) of committing a theft.

The laws themselves were readily open to abuse. Capital punishment was officially condemned by the Imperial authorities and no serf-owner was allowed to impose a death penalty on any offenders: he could, however, punish them so severely that they subsequently died and, provided that death did not occur either during or immediately after punishment, no action would be taken against him. The nobility were expected to provide a quota of recruits for the army from among their serfs but any peasant sent to Siberia would count as a military recruit, thus reducing the number of men to be found for the army. The serf-owner tended to deport infirm and inefficient peasants to Siberia in order to safeguard his own labour force. By the end of the eighteenth century this practice had become notorious and it was estimated that three-quarters of the unfortunate wretches

The luckless serf could find himself and his family driven ruthlessly to Siberia to further schemes of settlement.

90

sent to Siberia, the traditional home of penal settlements, died on the journey eastwards. Tsar Alexander, whose early years were rich in good intentions, suspended the serf-owner's rights of transportation soon after his accession. But the system was restored in 1806 under pressure from the landowners, who also used settlement in Siberia as a penal measure. Formal checks were thereafter imposed on the arrangements for transportation so as to curb the most flagrant abuses. An alternative method of punishment by which serfs were condemned to hard labour in the Navy was never popular with the authorities nor with the nobility. The Russian Admiralty was only interested in fit and able-bodied men and there was thus little opportunity for corruption. This strange variant on the press gang operated from 1765 until 1809, when it was abandoned from practical exigencies rather than humanitarian motives.

The first decade of the nineteenth century marked the zenith of serfdom in Russia. As a formal institution replacing older concepts of personal slavery which varied from region to region, serfdom dated only from the late fifteenth century. Its period of most rapid growth coincided with the years when enlightened ideas were spreading through some sections of the Russian nobility; the number of male serfs in the Empire appears almost to have doubled during Catherine II's reign, and this rapid increase was continued throughout the decade following her death. In 1796 Tsar Paul formally extended serfdom to the territories acquired by his mother's wars and diplomacy in the West and in the Caucasus; and in consequence the number of male serfs in the Empire rose from eight and a half million to ten and a half million in the following fifteen years. Since census returns for Russia at this time are so imprecise there must inevitably be some uncertainty over all estimates of the population, but it would seem that in 1812, on the eve of the Napoleonic invasion, fifty-eight per cent of the men living in European Russia were bound by direct obligations of serfdom: this was a higher proportion than at any time before or afterwards.

Yet by 1812 serfdom has passed its peak of influence within Russian society. Alexander I already accepted the principle that it was an institution unsuited to an increasingly industrialised economy: he forbade its introduction into Finland, Bessarabia, or any other territories annexed to the Empire during his reign; and he made no attempt, after the Napoleonic Wars, to restore serfdom in western Poland, where it was originally abolished by the French authorities in 1807. Once it was recognised that serfdom was economically wasteful and cumbersome, its importance as an institution began to decline. It had reached its fullest extent geographically in 1796; and within thirty years Tsar Nicholas I was apologising for it as 'the indubitable evil of Russian life', although he insisted that it was still essential as a basis of unity within the State.

Many foreign visitors to Russia regarded the terms 'serf' and 'slave' as synonymous; and, in a private letter soon after his accession, Alexander I wrote: 'The peasants of Russia are for the most part slaves: I do not need to dilate on the misery and misfortune of such a situation.' Yet technically there was a distinction between the Russian serf and the Negro slaves in America: the serfs believed they had rights of ownership over the land which they tilled (although in fact it belonged to the nobility) and they were thus free to enrich themselves by hard work provided that they had first fulfilled their obligations to their master. This opportunity to make his own holding yield both subsistence and profit saved the Russian serf from the moral degradation sensed by so many Negroes on the cotton plantations. Whether, in reality, the serf's small strip of land was of any value to him may be doubted: he tilled it with very primitive tools, and in most cases only during hours when he was not working for his lord. Moreover, the actual distribution of cultivable land was normally made by the collective body for the village (the *mir*), which had the right to re-distribute land among the peasants every few years so as to prevent any particular serf from enriching himself through the good fortune of possessing an especially fertile holding. But the very fact that there was a *mir* to safeguard land distribution, to retain a common store for the needy, and to establish a sense of community provided the serf with a status lacking in a purely slave society. That was, perhaps, the greatest difference of all between social servitude in Russia and in the southern states of the American Republic.

'Gambling for souls'; a caricature by Gustave Doré portraying Russian serfdom in 1855. Russian landowners are shown gambling with bundles of serfs, a practice even commoner in the early years of the century.

A village council (or *mir*) in a print of 1803.

The precise nature of service rendered by the serfs varied considerably from estate to estate and from one region of Russia to another. Basically they had to offer direct labour service (*barschina*) or money payment (*obrok*). The more exacting category was clearly *barschina*, which predominated in the richer agricultural regions, the 'Black Earth' zone south from Moscow to the Don and the Dnieper. Farther north (along the route followed by the French invaders in 1812) most serf labour was rendered by *obrok*, although sometimes the landowner insisted on payment in kind as well as cash, and occasionally serfs were expected to give limited labour services as well as offering *obrok*. The district around Smolensk was, however, a predominantly *barschina* zone; and the serfs whom Tolstoy mentions in his account of Prince Nicholas Bolkonsky's estate at Bald Hills would therefore have been expected to tender direct labour service. So they would, too, on Pierre's estates around Kiev; but at the beginning of Book VI we learn that Prince Andrew's serfs at Bogucharovo are in a different category: 'On one of his estates the three hundred serfs were liberated and became free agricultural labourers – this being one of the first examples of the kind in Russia. On other estates the serf's compulsory labour was commuted for a quit-rent' (i.e. *obrok*). Many of the more enlightened landowners were, in fact, following this type of practice and were finding – as Prince Andrew did – that modernisation brought its reward in better services and in personal loyalty.

There was no uniform pattern even of labour services. Most serf-owners required the peasants to work for them on three full days in every week, a principle tacitly accepted by Tsar Paul in 1797 and by

93

Michael Speransky, the reformer who codified Russia's legal system under Paul's two sons, Alexander and Nicholas. Frequently, however, serfs were expected to work for their master on four or five days a week, and sometimes, during haymaking or harvesting, six and occasionally seven. No distinction in working conditions was made between men and women in most regions of Russia, although women might be excused *barschina* for six weeks after childbirth. A working day was generally twelve hours in the summer and nine in the winter. Children of thirteen to seventeen normally had a more limited assignment of service than their elders: men continued to give *barschina* up to the age of fifty-five, and women to forty-five or fifty according to their state of health. A really enlightened proprietor would pay his peasants wages for any labour in excess of the regular *barschina*, but he was under no obligation to do so, nor was there any reason why, if he so desired, a proprietor should not insist on the serfs spending all their working days on his estate. Occasionally they were expected to render their labour service, not in the fields, but in the small factories attached to the estate or making cloth in their own cottages. The overseer of their work was the steward, who ran the noble's estate in his absence. Sometimes the landowner would be in residence for several months or longer – thus Tolstoy makes Prince Andrew pass the two years of Franco-Russian collaboration (1808–10) either on his father's lands at Bald Hills or supervising his own affairs and the lands held in trust for his son at Bogucharovo and Riazan – but normally it was only on the smaller properties that the landowner regularly took an active part in administering his estate.

A serf paying *obrok* rather than rendering *barschina* had far more personal freedom. His hours were not directly regulated by his master or by a steward. He could, in many cases, leave his village and seek occupation elsewhere provided that he had a written permit from his lord and, for periods of absence exceeding six months, from the government as well. In some areas (notably around St Petersburg and around Moscow after 1812) serfs on *obrok* would spend the summer in the cities working on the building projects; and the amount of *obrok* was assessed according to the wages the man received. The burden on an individual peasant could become formidable, especially if his obligations also involved contributions towards the salaries of the administrative officials on an estate, the maintenance of the village priest, and the upkeep of the church. Nevertheless, an *obrok* peasant regarded himself as more privileged than one on *barschina*: the threat of being transferred to labour service by an angry master was often an effective deterrent against failure to render to the lord all that was due to him.

The most unfortunate peasants of all were those who had been removed from their homes and holdings and assigned tasks as domestic servants of their master. Although there were many good lords who treated them with kindliness and understanding, they lost

Peasants at work in a typical, small, early nineteenth-century Russian factory.

virtually all individuality of person and their status was hardly distinguishable from that of a slave. Some lived in a compound close to their master's mansion, but many were housed under the same roof as the serf-owner, sometimes travelling in his retinue from one estate to another and from the countryside to the city. They waited at table, cooked his food, looked after his wine, cared for his horses and dogs, cleaned his residences; and their wives and daughters served as maids, nurses and seamstresses. Foreign travellers such as the Wilmot sisters and Ker Porter frequently commented with amazement on the sheer number of domestics in a noble household. Ker Porter described how:

The houses of the nobility are filled with these vassals, or sevants, both male and female, who line the halls, passages, and entrances of the rooms in splendid liveries. In almost every antechamber some of these domestics are placed, ready to obey the commands of their lord or his guests; and continually your ears are saluted with the theatrical call of 'Who waits?' when two or three run in at the instant, as promptly as I ever saw the gentlemen-in-waiting answer the like summons from the boards of Drury Lane or Covent Garden.

95

Wealthy landowners delighted in using their domestics as enter-
tainers as well as servants. Prince Alexander Kropotkin, for example,
had fifty domestics in Moscow and another seventy-five on his country
estate, where he maintained a large serf orchestra of which he was
extremely proud. The first two violinists were expected to make
music as their sole obligation of service, but the other performers all
carried out normal tasks within the household as well. Thus the
second butler was a flautist, a tailor played the French horn, and a
versatile footman performed on the trombone or bassoon and occasionally helped the string section on a violin. One unfortunate, nominally engaged as a confectionary pastrycook, was found to have less
musical talent than anticipated; and, having proved a disaster on
drums and trumpets, was accordingly drafted as a soldier. Kropotkin's private orchestra was regarded as a personal eccentricity, but
most of the top social families expected their domestics to show dramatic talent, and sometimes to sing and dance as well. Martha Wilmot's sense of humour was delighted by all this doubling-up of duties:
''Tis droll enough to be attended at Supper by the Hero of the piece
who has been strutting before your Eyes in Gilded robes etc. for half
the Evening,' she wrote, while commending the general level of the
entertainment.

Some domestic servants were, of course, abominably ill-used. A
few of the serf-owners possessed what were virtually harems, while
one of the earliest Serbian travellers claimed to have met a young and
pretty prostitute who was a domestic serf sent into the city to earn a
couple of roubles a year for her master. Martha Wilmot was a little
disappointed at the lack of extravagance in entertainment when she
dined in Moscow with Prince Nicholas Yusupov, who maintained a
private ballet company of serfs: on less constrained occasions the
Prince was in the habit of inviting his friends to a performance at
which the *corps de ballet*, on a given signal, would be expected to
remove their costumes and continue to dance naked before an appre-
ciative audience. Slapdash artistry was not tolerated; one nobleman
surprised his French guest by jumping up in the middle of an operatic
aria, slapping the face of the leading soprano, and promising her
that after the performance she would be taken to the stables and
soundly thrashed. It was this dependence upon the whims and tem-
pers of their masters (and often their mistresses too) which made life
so intolerable for the domestic serfs, especially in a society which
regarded corporal punishment as the natural corrective for way-
wardness among the lower orders.

Both Catherine the Great and Alexander were conscious of the
extent to which serfdom abused human dignity. Catherine in 1771
forbade the sale of serfs belonging to bankrupt nobles at public
auction, as she thought the spectacle was degrading: in the last
years of her reign, she changed her mind and permitted the sales
to be resumed, provided that the auctioneer did not actually use a

hammer. Alexander, on his accession, tried to stop newspapers from advertising the sale of serfs, but enterprising traders easily evaded his prohibition. At the beginning of the nineteenth century serfs were generally priced at between two hundred and five hundred roubles for a man and between fifty and one hundred roubles for a woman. Attractive girls at the Moscow market cost five hundred roubles at the time of Alexander's coronation, although ordinary housemaids were available at fifty roubles and were said to be cheaper and in better supply at Ivanovo, the textile centre a hundred and fifty miles north-east of the old capital. For particular talents high prices were asked, generally agreed discreetly and in private between vendor and purchaser. An advertisement in the newspaper *Moskovskie Vedomosti* throws an interesting light on how such transactions were conducted in the last years of the old century:

> For Sale: a girl of 16, a chambermaid who possesses a good voice and sings with skill; and therefore theatre lovers are hereby let know that the said girl can act cleverly in a dramatic role as well as keeping house and cooking meals. The price may be ascertained by inquiry from the Zobin House, near the Church of John the Baptist.

The price (and the fate) of the girl remains unknown; but a few years later an especially gifted serf-actress was bought for five thousand roubles, and was regarded as a good investment.

The accounts of foreign visitors give a misleading impression of affluence among members of the landowning classes at the start of the nineteenth century. Only sixteen per cent of the nobles owned more than one hundred serfs at the turn of the century and probably a third of the serf-owners had less than ten; and these proportions do not appear to have changed greatly in the course of Alexander's reign. There were, however, exceptions. The richest landowner of all was Count Nicholas Sheremetev, with 185,610 male and female serfs and 6,237,044 acres of land (an area equivalent in size to the combined counties of Yorkshire, Lancashire, Durham and Westmorland, and twice as large as the American state of Connecticut). The Count, who died in 1809, relied for his income mostly on *obrok*: he spent money happily on building palaces and on extravagant entertainments; and was so heavily in debt at the time of his death that his son found the whole of the annual income was absorbed by repayment of loans and by maintenance of the existing household. Prince Alexander Kurakin, an ambassador in Vienna and one of the leading Russian diplomats of the Napoleonic era, had a mere five thousand serfs but was as lavish in his habits as Sheremetev. Hence by the end of Alexander I's reign he was seven million roubles in debt, and was forced to mortgage all his lands to the government for thirty-seven years. Small wonder, if, with these examples before them, lesser nobles found themselves sinking more and more into debt. The hour of the despised merchant-class and the money-lenders was at hand;

by the end of the wars in Europe it had become clear that the one luxury the Russian nobility could not afford was the stagnant institution of serfdom.

Almost half of the peasants in Russia during Alexander I's reign were not technically serfs; but neither were they totally free men. Conquest and confiscation had made the Tsars of Russia massive landowners in their own right; the labourers on these government estates and on former church lands, secularised by Catherine II in 1764, were known as 'state peasants', and considered themselves socially more privileged than most of the serfs on the lands of the nobility. There were slightly more than five million male state peasants in Russia at the accession of Alexander and the figure increased steadily in the quarter of a century he was on the throne. The state peasants still had to bear obligations which were never imposed on the genuinely free inhabitants of the Empire. Until the last decades of the eighteenth century they had to obtain permits to undertake a journey away from their home district and they were expected to pay an exit permit for a daughter who wished to marry and settle in another region. Attempts were also made to prevent the peasants from drifting into the towns, finding work in commerce and industry. Most of these restrictions had been removed before 1812, or tacitly allowed to lapse. The peasants were, however, still bound to pay a heavy quota of direct taxes. Like the serfs, they were liable for the 'soul tax' (a poll-tax introduced by Peter the Great and levied on every male in the country except for the nobility, the clergy, and a few privileged persons). Moreover, most categories of state peasants were liable to pay a road tax, small duties to the provincial and district administrations, and a payment for services (a levy which replaced earlier obligations to provide the State with horses and cartage and to keep bridges in good repair). They were also obliged to contribute a quit-rent to the government for the land they tilled: this was the equivalent of the *obrok* paid by a serf to his master, but it was always a considerably smaller sum, even if the peasants complained that it rose sharply during the wars of Alexander's reign. As a final restriction on their liberties, the state peasants – again like the serfs – were liable to be recruited for the army, although there were particular categories to whom exemption was granted.

Despite this long list of taxes and duties, the position of a state peasant gave a man greater opportunity for advancement than any *obrok*-paying serf could ever enjoy; and it is not surprising that one of the categories of state peasants should have consisted entirely of serfs freed by command of the Tsar for distinction in the army. Naturally the state peasants were jealous of their rights and particularly proud of their independence from a master. Hence one of their chief fears was to find the land on which they lived handed over by the Tsar to a private land-owner, thereby lowering their own status and subjecting them directly to a lord or his steward. This process happened all too frequently during Paul's four and a half years on the throne.

There were, in addition to these state peasants, a number of men and women in Russia who were employed by the authorities and who constituted social groups of their own: workers in the Imperial stables or at the Imperial theatres; riders carrying official mail; foresters charged with responsibility for timber for the navy; and so on. Technically such groups were reckoned as peasants and generally appeared in this category on the census returns. Their obligations were closely defined, but many were exempt from the smaller taxes.

During the second half of Alexander's reign an attempt was made to introduce an entirely different system of land tenure to certain areas of Russia. The organiser of the scheme was one of the Tsar's closest advisers, General Alexei Arakcheev, an artilleryman with a gift for administration but notorious for his harsh discipline. With Alexander's enthusiastic patronage, Arakcheev established a network of settlements, mostly around Novgorod or in the Ukraine, where all farming, manufacturing and commerce were in the hands of the soldiery under strict discipline and regimentation. The earliest of these 'military colonies', as they were called, was set up between Smolensk and Minsk in 1810 but it was not until after the Napoleonic Wars (and especially between 1816 and 1821) that the system was used extensively. Only soldiers and their families were allowed to live within the military colonies: landowners whose estates were compulsorily purchased by the army were offered territory elsewhere and normally took their serfs with them; merchants and traders were given monetary compensation, which they invariably considered inadequate. By the end of Alexander's reign in 1825 some 750,000 people lived in these settlements. They had good housing, good schooling and the opportunity to increase food supplies, as the methods of cultivation were better than elsewhere. But the system was unpopular: landowners disliked 'unfair' competition for agricultural produce; the settlers resented the brutal methods of their commandants, many of whom thought farming a poor substitute for campaigning; and intelligent observers among the nobility were alarmed at the way in which the colonies became autocracies within an autocracy, fearing their potential political impact under some future tsar of weak character. Although the military colonies excited much interest among foreign visitors, they were regarded with little sympathy by Alexander's successor, Nicholas I: and after a mutiny in 1831 they were modified out of all recognition.

The experiment of the military colonies failed because there was no place for it in the Russian way of life. Serfdom was an evil institution and ill-suited to a changing economy, as most thoughtful Russians recognised even during Alexander's reign; but at least it was founded on a traditional relationship between master and servant. The military colonies made the mistake of confusing this

Above Russian mail carrier; a state employed peasant.

Right Count A. A. Arakcheev, one of Alexander I's principle advisers, and the man responsible for the development of Russian artillery and the military colonies. He was loathed by the serfs for his brutal methods: Etching by Utkin.

bond with the obligations that a private soldier had towards his officers and that the officers themselves felt towards their commander-in-chief. By Alexander's reign the army was as much a separate Estate as the peasantry: it did not take kindly to having its swords beaten into plough-shares and its spears into pruning-hooks. A victorious soldiery tends to look elsewhere among the Old Testament prophets for solace and inspiration.

The future Tsar
Alexander among a
group of cadets at
Peterhof, during the
reign of Catherine the
Great. These young
men would all be of
noble family.

4 Sons of Suvorov

By THE END of the eighteenth century Russian society, with its Table of Ranks and its enforced subjection of individual liberties to imperial authority, was excessively militarised. In spirit, however, it had never become militaristic. Although the nobility were expected to provide an officer class for the army, the holding of a commission did not in itself guarantee any particular social standing, as it did in most of central and western Europe. Hence, while it was common for landowners to serve for comparatively brief periods in the army, the great Russian families supplied remarkably few career officers – a marked contrast to the aristocracy in Prussia, the Austrian Empire and pre-revolutionary France. For their senior commanders the Tsars long relied on a substantial leavening of foreign-born professional soldiers, although these 'Germans' (as, irrespective of their origin, they were invariably called) were never popular. It was only in the closing decades of the old century that victories by 'true sons of Russia' began to fire patriotic pride, making service as an officer in the elite regiments an attractive ambition for the younger generation. It was during the struggles against the French in the Napoleonic era that the finest traditions of the Imperial Russian Army were shaped. A military mystique was in the making.

Until Peter the Great's reign the Muscovite State had gone to war relying for success upon the sheer numerical strength of a largely untrained militia, supplemented by irregular Cossack horsemen from the Don Basin and other primitive regions along the borders with Asia. Peter, however, ruthlessly swept away the old methods of levying troops and substituted for them the nucleus of a standing army. By 1721 he had organised for Russia a military establishment based upon fifty-six infantry regiments (of which the two most renowned units were the Semeonovsky Guards and the Preobrazhenski Grenadiers), thirty-three cavalry regiments and one regiment of artillery. When he died five years later the army numbered 130,000 men. They were armed with flintlocks and bayonets which were originally imported from England but subsequently manufactured

by the armaments works at the city of Tula, where cannon had been cast for the artillery since the seventeenth century. During the Seven Years War (1756–63) the fire-power of the Russian guns had already won grudging respect from Frederick II of Prussia.

Basically the structure of the Russian army changed little during the second half of the eighteenth century. It grew considerably, however, and so, too, did the war potential of the Empire as a whole. In 1767, for example, Tula was manufacturing 30,000 muskets a year and it was calculated that the army had more than 13,000 pieces of artillery (some of them admittedly old and too well-worn). On several occasions in Catherine II's reign, the Empress had over half a million men under arms (including 40,000 Cossack horsemen) but there was still a large untapped reserve of manpower among the peasants, and at the time of Catherine's death still only one man in every thirty-six within her Empire was actually serving as a soldier. When it is remembered that the army had to be ready to fight on three fronts – in the Central European plain, against Turkey, and against the tribes of the Caucasus – it is clear that the number of troops available for concentration at any one point along Russia's huge frontiers was always unavoidably small. Nevertheless, the transformation of the Russian army from a largely feudal institution to a modern force remained one of the remarkable military developments of the century.

The rank and file of the army were recruited by a quota system from the serfs and peasantry. At irregular intervals the authorities in St Petersburg informed the village communities of the number of conscripts required and these were then selected by the *mir*, under the general direction of the landowner or his steward. Over the whole century following Peter's death the recruit summons went out, on the average, once every two years; but the proportion of conscripts varied according to the state of political emergency: two men in every five hundred serfs in time of secure peace (a rare condition) and one man in every twenty during the crisis years 1812–14. State peasants liable for service were conscripted directly by a recruiting officer. There were numerous methods of evading service, ranging from the buying of substitutes and the transference of a likely conscript from one estate to another on the approach of the recruiting authorities, down to deliberate maiming of the body by the unfortunate who was faced with military service. The army accepted the system by which substitutes were purchased, for it cared only about numbers and not the rights of the individual; but it dealt drastically with any person found inflicting a wound upon himself, sometimes by ignoring the injury and forcing the conscript to serve in a punishment battalion, and often by a severe whipping and – if the unfortunate cripple survived it – by a long term of hard labour as well. Since the peasant felt a natural instinct to defend his homeland from the invader, there was much less evasion of duty during the second half of 1812

Grenadiers, Musketeers and Chasseurs of the Russian army.

than in earlier years; but once the Grand Army was expelled from the Russian Empire, all the old abuses speedily crept back again. There was, in general, little enthusiasm among the masses for carrying war into foreign lands.

Occasionally army service must have come as a relief for a serf who constantly incurred the displeasure of a cruel master; but the fact that conscripts were willing to mutilate themselves and risk severe punishment shows how deeply the peasants detested the prospect of being turned into soldiers. Quite apart from a natural reluctance to have their lives thrown away in some senseless campaign, there were two principal causes of anguish; length of service, and intensive discipline. Recruits were taken from their families and required to serve for twenty-five years: unless they came from the vicinity of one of the great cities, it was extremely unlikely that, during this whole period, they would see again their home or their parents and friends. Ker Porter describes how rapidly a change would be made in their appearance and bearing so that within a few days of their arrival at the barracks they were cleaned up, booted, shaved and taught to march smartly rather than to slouch. Once they could hold themselves as soldiers they were provided with muskets and long greatcoats and left to the mercies of a drill-sergeant, who would use his swagger-cane ruthlessly in order to provoke a response from men who had so recently been boorish yokels. Ker Porter believed that the Russian temperament lent itself to obedience and discipline:

'Taken from a state of slavery,' he wrote, 'they [the Russian soldiers] have no idea of acting for themselves when any of their superiors are by; hence, they are as ready to receive all outward impressions as a piece of clay in the modeller's hands; and that the hands of the modellers are not very idle, they daily feel on their heads and shoulders enforced by the cane.'

The intensity of punishment in the Russian army owed much to Prussian practices. Both countries, for example, used the penalty of *spits-ruten*: defaulters were stripped to the waist and dragged, in manacles, through columns of soldiers armed with birches or whips. Major-General Sir Robert Wilson, with his knowledge of the brutality in the British army and navy at this time, thought that Russian discipline was just and beneficial; he actually committed himself to the surprising statement that 'Punishment is not so frequent as in other armies, nor is it very severe', and he drew a happy picture of the well-meaning Russian regimental officers treating their men 'with peculiar kindness'. Much of the factual evidence runs against Wilson on this count: for example, General Arakcheev, who was Minister of War from 1808 to 1810, once sentenced forty trouble-makers to a thousand lashes; and Colonel Schwarz, commander of one of the crack Guards regiments, provoked a mutiny by ordering the flogging for trivial offences of men decorated with the highest order for bravery. On the other hand, it is of course true that Tsarist officials,

Типы русских солдат в 1812 г.

civil as well as military, relied to an unusual extent upon the inflic-
tion of pain as a guarantee of authority. 'Nearly the whole of Russia
groaned under blows', wrote one of Arakcheev's junior officers,
looking back on this period from later in the century.

Since Russia was distant, vast and remote, few military authorities
in western Europe knew much about its army at the turn of the
century. Some of the Austrian commanders had served Catherine
II against the Turks and there was a close Austro-Russian collaboration – often singularly disastrous – in northern Italy during the
campaign of 1799. The Prussians retained horrific memories of ill-
discipline during the Seven Years War when the Cossack squadrons
had committed bestialities which scandalised the Russian regular
officers. But to the British – and, indeed, to the French – the Russian
army remained a legendary force, respected for its size rather than
its fighting qualities. Inevitably, the English looked in the first in-
stance to the accounts of travellers, giving pride of place to Robert
Wilson, who had toured the Russian garrison cities as a Colonel on a
special mission in 1807 and who established a warm friendship with
Tsar Alexander.

Soviet historians, commemorating the 150th anniversary of Napoleon's invasion, roundly condemn Wilson as 'a spy' who 'deliberately
distorted the facts'. It is true that in later years his writing was
marred by sensational prejudices, but when he published his *Brief*

Remarks on the Character and Composition of the Russian Army in 1810, his narrative glowed with a disingenuous enthusiasm for its subject. It was a book which had considerable influence, not only in England; a copy even found its way into Napoleon's library and was consulted by the Emperor and his staff during the planning of the 1812 campaign. No one who read it could fail to be impressed by the stamina and fortitude of the Russian army.

Robert Wilson was himself a cavalryman, but he particularly admired the bearing of the Tsar's infantrymen:

The infantry is generally composed of athletic men between the ages of 18 and 40 endowed with great bodily strength, but generally of short stature, with martial countenance and complexion; inured to the extremes of weather and hardship; to the worst and scantiest food; to marches for days and nights, of four hours repose and six hours progress; accustomed to laborious toils, and the carriage of heavy burdens; ferocious but disciplined; obstinately brave and susceptible of enthusiastic excitements; devoted to their sovereign, their chief and their country. Religious without being weakened by superstition; patient, docile, and obedient; possessing all the energetic characteristics of a barbarian people, with the advantages engrafted by civilization.

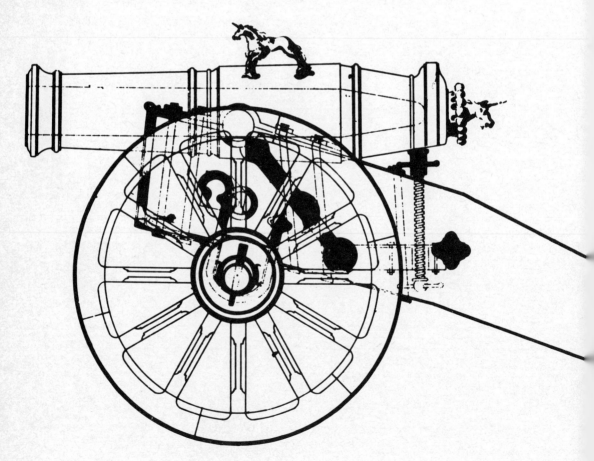

He was also impressed by the splendid condition of the cavalry horses and by the mobility of the field guns:

No troops can and do defend ground in retreat better than the Russians. Their artillery is so well horsed, so nimbly and so handily worked, that it bowls over almost all irregularities of surface with an ease, lightness, and velocity that give it great superiority.

Other observers were more critical than Wilson. In the same year that *Brief Remarks* was published, Edward Clarke, the first Professor of Mineralogy at Cambridge, printed an account of a journey he had made in 1800 from St Petersburg to the Crimea, in the course of which he was shown around the arms factory at Tula. Wilson, the professional soldier, praised the high quality of Russian weapons; Clarke, on the other hand, was unimpressed. He described what he had seen in Tula:

The machinery is ill constructed and worse preserved. Everything seemed out of order. Workmen, with long beards, stood staring at each other, wondering what was to be done next; while their intendants or directors were drunk or asleep. Notwithstanding all this, they pretended to issue from the manufactory . . . thirteen hundred muskets in a week. But the name of musket is almost all that connects the appearance with the reality. It is wonderful any troops can use them: besides being clumsy and heavy, they miss fire five times out of six, and are liable to burst whenever discharged.

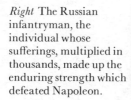

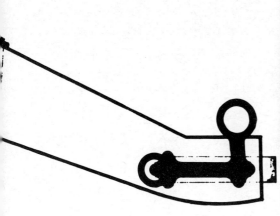

Left The Russian 'Unicorn' cannon, manufactured at Tula.

Right The Russian infantryman, the individual whose sufferings, multiplied in thousands, made up the enduring strength which defeated Napoleon.

The evidence of the bitter struggle which Russia waged against Napoleon suggests that, while the cannons cast at Tula were of high quality, Clarke was fully justified in deriding the muskets. Significantly one of the chief requests for military aid made by the Russians to the British after the Napoleonic invasion singled out the need for reliable infantry weapons; and 50,000 English muskets were gratefully unloaded at St Petersburg early in October 1812, the first of several consignments from London.

Almost every account of travels in Russia during this period commented favourably on the most famous – and most feared – troops in the Tsar's army, the Cossacks. The majority of Cossack soldiers came from the lower reaches of the river Don or from the Volga: they had shed the wilder habits of their ancestors, the horsemen of the Mongolian steppe; but they retained considerable privileges and customs, including the right to assemble in an oligarchic 'host' of their own and to serve as auxiliaries under their recognised commanders. Until 1754 the senior Cossack officers were elected, but by the end of the century they were appointed by the Tsar and his military advisers in St Petersburg. The Don Cossacks, unlike the Cossack communities in the Urals and eastern Siberia, had become integrated into the Russian order of society, their officers generally reckoned to possess the 'rank' of gentry and therefore the right to own serfs. The Cossack army was led by an *Ataman*, or Governor, whose dignity was treated with respect by the Tsar and his administrative officials.

Ker Porter, as an artist, was fascinated by the appearance of the Cossacks as soon as he arrived in Russia:

The troops which first strike the eye of a stranger on entering St Petersburg are the Cossacks; and certainly more curious objects cannot be imagined. Their persons, air, and appointments and the animals on which they are mounted, seem so totally at variance, that you can hardly suppose a reason for so unequal a union. The men are robust and fit for service: their horses appear completely the reverse: mean in shape and slouching in motion, every limb speaks of languor, and every moment you expect to see them drop down dead under their heavy burden: but so false are these shows, that there is not a more hardy animal existing; it will travel incalculable journeys, and remain exposed to the heat or cold, day and night, without manifesting any sense of inconvenience.

He thought that their uniform was 'the most soldierlike and serviceable dress I have met with in any country' because it was strictly utilitarian while, at the same time, looking impressive:

Their dress is military and useful, consisting of a close dark blue jacket and very large full trousers, under which they wear drawers and boots. Their head is covered with a high black cap of sheepskin: a red bag hangs from its top ornamented with a chain of white worsted lace and tassels: a red stripe, rather broad, runs along the outside of the trousers, as well as a

Image captions (left to right, top row then bottom row):
Officiers des Cosaques du Don. *Cosaque de la Mer Noire.* *Cosaque d'Irkoutsk.* *Chef des Tartares d'Oczakow.*
Chef des Baskirs. *Tartare Tonguse.* *Cosaque de la Siberie.* *Kirguis.*

A Paris chez Basset, Md d'Estampes, rue St Jacques au coin de celle des Mathurins No 64. *Déposé a la Direction Générale de l'Imprimerie et de la Librairie*

Cossack cavalry
from different regions
of Russia.

cord of the same colour around the cape and sleeves. A single row of buttons closes the jacket at the breast. A broad leather belt, containing cartridges, and to which is suspended a light sabre, confines their waists. Their principal weapons are a pike about eight feet long and a pair of pistols. A black belt crosses their left shoulder, to which is attached a sort of tin cartouch box, holding ammunition and surmounted with a ramrod. An uncouth saddle is bound on the horse, somewhat like a double pillow, under which is a square piece of oil cloth painted in various colours. . . . Some of the men wear moustachios, and some dispense with that fierce appendage.

Ker Porter's admiration for the Cossacks was shared by Robert Wilson, whose account of their appearance is not dissimilar. He adds, however, some comments on their manoeuvrability in the field:

Mounted on a very little, ill-conditioned, but well bred horse, which can walk at the rate of five miles an hour with ease, or in his speed dispute the race with the swiftest . . . armed with the lance, a pistol in his girdle and a sword, he never fears a competitor in single combat. . . . They act in dispersion and, when they do re-unite to charge, it is not with a systematic formation, but *en masse*, or what in Germany is called swarm attack. Dexterous

in the management of a horse that is guided only by the snaffle, they can twist and bend their course through the most intricate country at full speed.

While it was generally accepted that the common soldier was obedient and tenacious, foreign commentators frequently doubted the ability of the Russian officer class and the ingenuity of its senior commanders. Even Wilson, who was spoilt and flattered by army society during his first visit to Russia, complained that one of the 'defects of education' was to produce 'indolent habits' among the Russian officers when not on actual duty. They liked, Wilson says, to 'sleep after food' and disliked to walk or ride far: 'At Petersburg or Moscow no person of rank moves on foot, and a journey of fifty miles on horseback would be an expedition for the city's talk.' He claimed, however, that though the high nobility was 'accustomed to every luxury' they were able to 'encounter the rudeness of the most severe campaigns'. Other foreign soldiers visiting Russia, especially Germans who had gone into exile rather than accept Napoleonic rule, thought the officers too fond of comfort and too inclined to waste precious hours in drinking, gambling or sheer natural sloth. To some extent these criticisms were shared both by Tsar Paul and by Tsar

The speed and manoeuvrability of the Cossack horsemen was one of the greatest assets of the Russian troops.

Alexander. When he was heir to the throne, Paul slavishly copied outmoded Prussian methods of drill and command, a practice he carried, after his accession, from his palace at Gatchina to the parade grounds of Petersburg; and Alexander so lacked confidence in Russian judgements that he tended to turn for advice to Austrian or Prussian 'experts', many of them mere paper strategists and unable to understand the strange character of warfare across the great expanses of the Russian plain.

Alexander's doubts were not justified. Although Russia did not possess military academies of the stature of the French *École Militaire* or the Gross Lichterfelde cadet school in Prussia, attempts had been made for seventy years before Alexander's accession to provide the sons of the nobility with an education which would fit them for service in the crack regiments. As early as 1731 a cadet corps institute was set up in which young nobles might enlist as soon as they were thirteen years old: three hundred and sixty cadets were housed in the Menschikov Palace at St Petersburg and were given a sound general education as well as practical military training. Under Catherine II this system was extended: in 1766 the Land Cadet Corps College provided schooling for the sons of the nobility between the ages of six and twenty; and by the later years of her reign the school for artillery cadets at Shlyaktherny was recognised as an institution of considerable social standing. The Shlyaktherny cadets enjoyed a prestige which in other countries was generally reserved, as of right, for the cavalry. Quite apart from instruction in riding, fencing, land surveying and applied mathematics, the students were well-grounded in Russian, German and French and acquired some

A young Russian officer is squeezed into his uniform by his valets, to the apparent alarm of a lady onlooker.

knowledge of European literature and history. In a country where schools were few and private tutors of variable quality, the educational value of the military academies was considerable; and it is not surprising that many of their pupils, after attaining field-rank in the army, transferred to the diplomatic corps or to civil administration.

However, during Paul's reign, the morale of the officer corps and the level of training in the military academies deteriorated disastrously. There were three main reasons for the decline: excessive centralisation and uniformity; capricious promotions, announced in order to satisfy the Tsar's whim of the moment; and the enforced retirement of senior officers reared in a Russian tradition of service and unwilling to Prussianise their regiments. General Serge Andolenko, a modern historian of the Russian army, has calculated that during the comparatively brief reign of Paul, seven marshals, over three hundred generals and two thousand other officers were excluded from service ('put on half-pay', as it were). This development was particularly ill-timed. It coincided with the creation in revolutionary France of 'citizen armies', offering opportunity for merit to be recognised and stimulating among junior officers a passionate desire for military glory. While the French were thus shaping the nucleus of Napoleon's Grand Army, Russian military potential was allowed to waste away because of the personal whims of an unstable sovereign. Paul's reign was a disastrous interlude for tsardom: his Prussianising military affectations almost cost his Empire her hard-won status as a Great Power.

The dominant ideas on strategy and tactics remained, however, wholly Russian in origin. Two commanders of the front rank shaped military thought among the officer corps in the second half of the century: Marshal Pyotr Rumyantsev (1725–96); and Marshal Alexander Suvorov (1729–1800). Rumyantsev was said to be a bastard son of Peter the Great, and his character certainly seems at times to have been lit by flashes of Peter's wayward genius. He distinguished himself first in the Seven Years War, but it was his triumphs against the Turks in 1769–70 which assured him of a high place in the chronicles of warfare, if only because his troops were the earliest Russians to reach the river Danube. Yet Rumyantsev's influence was to prove more enduring than his actual victories: he was responsible, to a greater extent than any other soldier, for establishing the basic strategic principle of Russian policy, the desirability of waging a war of movement rather than the static concentration of great armies in a limited arena. The sullen emptiness of the steppe-land, where towns were often fifty miles apart and settlements marked as villages on a map were no more than collections of huts, imposed a distinctive character on warfare in the great plains of Eastern Europe and Russia. No general would seek to fight in the Ukraine or Bessarabia or White Russia as he would among the hills of Bohemia-Moravia or the varying contours of Italy,

Previous page The Battle of Eylau painted by Gros. A triumphant Napoleon sports the arms of Poland to the obviously joyful inspiration of his noble Polish brothers-in-arms.

Count Suvorov sketched by Gillray *c.* 1799. The Russian General acquired the status of a legendary hero in his own lifetime.

for example. Operations against the Turks or against any invader of the Russian homeland inevitably bore a closer resemblance to the pursuit of an enemy fleet at sea than to the methodical advance of an eighteenth-century army from fortress to fortress in western Europe. 'The objective is not the occupation of a geographical position but the destruction of enemy forces,' Rumyantsev once declared; and this maxim, first enunciated in the 1770s, has remained valid for every successful Russian commander, whether in the army of the tsars or in the Red Army of the twentieth century. It was fundamental to the strategy of Marshal Kutuzov in 1812.

Suvorov is the most legendary of all Russia's generals. He came from one of the families of the lesser nobility, with lands near Novgorod. Despite his good birth, he enlisted as a private in the Semeonovsky Guards in 1745 and served six years in the ranks before being commissioned. In this way he gained a background of sympathy and understanding for the soldiery that chiefly explains the remarkable hold his memory commands on the loyalty of successive generations of Russians. In forty years as a commander it is calculated that he won sixty-three victories and never suffered a major defeat: he fought in the Seven Years War and against the Turks in 1774 and from 1787 to 1792; he helped quell the rebellion of serfs under Pugachev in 1773, and he captured Warsaw from the Polish rebels in 1794. Probably his greatest feat was the storming of the Turkish fortress of Ismail on the Danube delta in December 1791; but his most famous achievements were the victories against the French in northern Italy in 1799 and his subsequent passage of the Alps, where he inspired his men to scale the St Gothard in a vain effort to thrust forwards towards France and Paris itself. Suvorov was in his seventieth year during this campaign against the French and he died a few months later: but his reputation survived; and so, above all, did his teaching.

While Rumyantsev's ideas were primarily concerned with grand strategy, Suvorov concentrated on building up a communal spirit among his men and on inducing his subordinate officers to take rapid and unexpected decisions on the battlefield. He thought that tactical surprise was no less essential for success in a campaign than strategic surprise; and he summarised his principles of warfare in a laconic phrase – 'Intuition, Rapidity, Impact'. It seemed to him essential for an officer to be able to assess a situation swiftly, decide on an objective, and then concentrate all his resources on attaining it. Like Napoleon, he believed that opportunities are created by luck but exploited by intelligence. 'Fortune goes past like a flash of lightning,' he told his troops, 'Seize her by the hair, for she will never come back to you.' As a general rule of strategy, he maintained that a commander-in-chief should seek, not merely to break through the enemy line, but to strike at the very point where a reversal would endanger the whole enemy position. It was through such methods that Napoleon gained his most impressive triumphs, including the defeat of the Austro-Russian forces at Austerlitz; and it is interesting that the two greatest soldiers of successive generations should, independently, have evolved such a similar theory of war.

Suvorov and Napoleon never faced each other in battle. During the months that Suvorov was winning his victories in Italy, General Bonaparte was fighting in Egypt and Syria, and the defence of France was left to Joubert, Soult, Macdonald and Massena. And by the time Napoleon embarked on the Marengo campaign, Tsar Paul had made peace between Russia and France and Suvorov himself lay dying in St Petersburg. They buried him in the crypt of the Annunciation at the Nevsky Monastery, his tomb marked by an epitaph eloquent in its brevity, 'Here Lies Suvorov.' He bequeathed a double legacy to Russia: a belief in a particular way of waging war; and a 'school' of generals, who had served under him against the Turks or against the French and who were confident that the Tsar's army must follow his teachings if the Napoleonic threat was to be overcome. Chief among these disciples of Suvorov were Michael Kutuzov (1745–1813) and Prince Bagration (1765–1812), both of whom were idolised by the armies they commanded and rightly

Kutuzov's portrait, hanging in the Winter Palace's military gallery, shows him in triumphant command, surrounded by smaller portraits of the eight generals whose roles in the 1812 campaign were so greatly overshadowed in the popular imagination by Kutuzov's rocklike final stand.

given pride of place among Russia's military leaders in Tolstoy's novel.

After the Turkish campaign of 1791–92 Suvorov had said of Kutuzov, 'He commanded my left flank but he was my right arm.' The two men understood each other well: they shared a simple and unsophisticated way of life, characteristically Russian in its virtue and vices. Neither of them possessed the flattery of a courtier, and both were inclined to express themselves in proverbs and fables, showing a gift of imagery which appealed to the common soldiers in their armies. They had fought together at Alushta in 1774, where a Turkish bullet had destroyed Kutuzov's right eye, and at the siege of Ismail in 1791, where Kutuzov's bravery had won him Suvorov's commendation. But Kutuzov was more devious and slyer than Suvorov had ever been: he hated being called on to give a definite verdict on reports submitted to him by subordinate officers; and he was always reluctant to commit himself so far as to sign any formal order. Outwardly he showed those defects of indolence which General Wilson so deplored in the Russian officers: at the age of sixty Kutuzov already seemed prematurely old, liking good food, good wine, and all the comfort of easy chairs or soft beds. He was too fat to stay long in the saddle and preferred to inspect his men in a carriage rather than on horseback. In 1805 it was uncertain whether he spent more of the day asleep or awake: by 1812 there was no doubt at all that sleep had won. As a young man the ladies of St Petersburg had found him an attractive war-hero; and he still enjoyed female companionship, with a happy disregard for rank or social status. To some extent Kutuzov played on his eccentricities, taking care to hide his shrewdness and sometimes surprising those who had not known him in earlier years by an unexpected display of ruthless vengeance. He was not such a versatile commander as Suvorov, for he was at his best in the steppe-land and could never have contemplated a march through the Swiss Alps. But he was resilient and tenacious, a commander for the long campaign not for the parade-ground; his qualities did not naturally endear him either to Tsar Paul or to Tsar Alexander.

Prince Bagration was a very different type of commander from Kutuzov. He came from a high-ranking Caucasian family, with estates in Georgia, and he entered the Russian army in 1772, serving against the Turks and the Polish rebels before gaining an international reputation for his daring in northern Italy and Switzerland in 1799. 'My Bagration possesses a spirited presence, skill, courage and good fortune,' Suvorov declared. He could well have added to the list ambition and recklessness, so that at times Bagration seemed a fire-eating braggart. Generally he was a man of dignity, massively taciturn, but his nerves were sometimes held so tautly that they broke unexpectedly over trifles and he could lose his temper on a grand scale. He showed a sound strategic sense, rather than an

The commanders of the Tsar

Right Prince Bagration
(1765–1812).

Left Matvei Platov
(1751–1818).

Right Ludgig
Wittgenstein
(1769–1843).

Below Barclay de Tolly
(1761–1818).

Below Levin Bennigsen
(1745–1826).

original one; but his reputation was growing steadily throughout the first half of Alexander's reign. The soldiery admired his gifts of leadership and nicknamed him *Bog-Rati-On* ('He is God of the Army') and his qualities were much respected by the nobility. Tolstoy, drawing upon the diary of a young student (S. P. Zhikharev), gives a vivid account of the English Club's dinner in honour of Bagration in March 1806 in which he emphasises Bagration's embarrassed shyness at the courtesies shown to him. There is a long description of the dinner and the subsequent entertainment in Ker Porter's *Travelling Sketches in Russia* – for he, too, was a guest at the banquet – and it is clear that Bagration was treated by the Moscow nobility as a military hero without equal in the Empire at that time, 'an honour to human nature', as Ker Porter described him. Whether he had the right temperament for overall command may be doubted, for he lacked Suvorov's mastery of military theory and Kutuzov's natural craftiness; but he was a magnetic personality who could fire his men to attempt the impossible, just as Ney and Murat were able to do at the peak of their influence in Napoleon's Grand Army.

There were, of course, other close companions and pupils of Suvorov who distinguished themselves in the campaigns of 1805–7 and 1812–14. Among them were General Miloradovich, General Raevski, and the Cossack commander, Matvei Platov. But there was also a group of senior officers who had never been members of the 'Suvorov School', though some had served under him. The most prominent soldier in this category was General Barclay de Tolly (1761–1818), who was born in Lithuania but was descended from a Scottish soldier who had settled in Russia in the seventeenth century. Barclay was not an impressive leader and was never popular with his fellow officers or with the men (who referred to him as 'Old Bark and No Bite'). Tsar Alexander had a high regard for Barclay's administrative skill and sense of order, but he was a cautious man with a predisposition for retreat and it is only with the passage of time that the wisdom of many of his judgements has become apparent.

Two of the other senior commanders in the Tsar's army were non-Russian by origin, Levin Bennigsen (1745–1826) and Ludwig Wittgenstein (1769–1843). Both had a Germanic background which did not endear them to the increasingly xenophobic rank and file, nor to the nationally-conscious junior officers. Bennigsen was born in Hanover and only entered Russian service, with field-rank, when he was twenty-eight. No-one doubted his bravery in battle, but he was a clumsy strategist and his career was hampered by Alexander's knowledge of the prominent part he had played in the murder of Tsar Paul. Wittgenstein had no such impediment to advancement: he came from the Westphalian nobility but, as his father had served in Catherine II's army, he was technically Russian in upbringing although his character and interests were as Germanic as

Bennigsen's. His military talents were limited: he was always willing to accept responsibility but, perhaps for this very reason, he was slow to show individual initiative. All three of these commanders – Barclay, Bennigsen, and Wittgenstein – were more orthodox than the 'Suvorov School', and they were therefore heard with greater respect by the conventionally-trained Alexander than were Bagration and Kutuzov.

Tsar Alexander's views mattered considerably; for, in the last resort, military policy in Russia still depended upon the will of the sovereign. It was not until 1802 that a Ministry of War was set up in St Petersburg, and even then the military staff continued to regard themselves as solely responsible to the Tsar himself (a misguided concept of loyalty which was only finally broken during the army reforms of 1867). Alexander had the ultimate right to determine the disposition of the troops and the direction of strategy. As a Grand Duke he had been trained for military command, mostly under the Prussianised influence of his father's Gatchina battalions. He took his soldierly duties so seriously that it was inconceivable he would allow his generals to position the army for war without asserting his opinions on the conduct of operations. No sovereign of Russia had led his troops into battle since Peter the Great's death, but this was largely because for sixty-nine of the seventy-six years which separate the reigns of Peter and Alexander the throne of Russia had been occupied by a woman ruler. The young Tsar was not likely to remain in St Petersburg while the rulers of Austria, Prussia and France marched at the head of their regiments.

When Russia went to war against France in 1805, Tsar Alexander set out for Berlin and ultimately for his first campaign, in Moravia. He was then twenty-seven years old. So had Napoleon been on receiving command of the Army of Italy in 1796; but he was already an experienced veteran. Alexander in 1805 knew the textbooks and all the theory of battle. It was Russia's tragedy that he did not perceive the cruellest schooling was yet to come.

5 'Power is my mistress'

Napoleon Bonaparte.

IN 1805 NAPOLEON STOOD at the pinnacle of his greatness as statesman and soldier. He had been proclaimed Emperor of the French in May 1804 and consecrated by Pope Pius VII at an imperial coronation in Notre Dame on 2 December, placing the crown on his own head, as Charlemagne had done ten centuries previously. By now most of Western Europe and the Italian peninsula acknowledged his sovereignty, directly and indirectly. Millions of people, within and beyond the old territorial frontiers of France, enjoyed the real advantages of his paternal protection – orderly government and administration, respect for the family, codes of law which emphasised the sanctity of property and guaranteed equality of rights for all citizens. The cost of these gains was, however, almost endless war. France had fought against the First Coalition (Austria, Britain, Naples, the Netherlands, Prussia and Spain) from 1792 to 1797 and against the Second Coalition (Austria, Britain, Naples, Portugal, Russia and Turkey) from 1798 to 1801; and even during the interludes between coalitions the war had continued against Britain, except for fourteen months of uneasy truce in 1802–3. Now, in 1805, the diplomats of London, Vienna and St Petersburg were busy weaving a Third Coalition against the overlord of Europe. Once again the thirty-six year old Emperor was stirring the imagination of young conscripts with the thrill of marching beside destiny to new triumphs. 'Power is my mistress,' he declared, 'I have worked too hard at her conquest to allow anyone to take her from me.'

On his own admission, the French armies of 1805 were the finest troops Napoleon ever led. Over twelve years of warfare enabled him to form divisions comprising a sound balance of hardened veterans and eager recruits; and he was able to draw on experienced commanders who were not, as yet, weary of campaigning. In May 1804 he had revived the ancient dignity of 'Marshal of France' and bestowed the title on eighteen of his commanders in arms, later promoting other generals to join the original paladins. Seven of them were to distinguish themselves in the War of the Third Coalition:

Overleaf The Battle of Borodino painted by Lejeune. The incident taking place in the foreground is the fatal wounding of Bagration.

125

Three of the leaders of Napoleon's finest army:
Right Marshal Davout, a strict disciplinarian of the Grand Army.
Below left Baron Gerard's portrait of Joachim Murat, French Marshal, King of Naples, and brother-in-law of Napoleon.
Below right Marshal Ney, the 'bravest of the brave' in Napoleon's phrase.

Berthier, his incomparable chief-of-staff; Bernadotte, tall and brave and dashing, a man who had risen from Sergeant to General in four years; Soult, another ex-Sergeant rapidly promoted to field rank, no less courageous and imperturbable than Bernadotte though lacking the swagger of his personality; Lannes, a natural swordsman, aggressive and nimble but patient in defence; Ney, the impetuous red-headed seeker after glory, quick-witted and resolute; Davout, austere and methodical, peering short-sightedly over his maps through specially designed spectacles; and Murat, a brother-in-law to Napoleon, and in his own right a Byron among the cavalry commanders of Europe. With such leaders for his men, Napoleon felt confident of meeting the challenge from the Austrians and Russians, and indeed from any other of the old professional armies of Europe; for none could match the French spirit of initiative and inner confidence.

Throughout the summer of 1805 it was clear that war would not long be delayed. Napoleon had known that the British and Russians were negotiating an alliance during the previous winter and the Russians subsequently held talks with both the Swedes and the Austrians. It was in fact the Austrians who began military operations by marching against French positions in southern Germany during the second week of September.

Allied war aims were confused. The Austrians simply wished to recover their lost primacy in Germany and Italy. Alexander brought Russia into the war for more complex reasons. He too wished the French to evacuate the German and Italian lands but he saw the campaign as a means of laying the foundations of 'a new code for the law of nations'; and he looked forward to the establishment of an equitable state-system in the heart of Europe.

Neither the British nor the Austrians entirely accepted Alexander's ambitious programme: they were more concerned with the practicable problem of inflicting a defeat on Napoleon. While the British concentrated on destroying French naval power, it was understood that the continental allies would advance against the French positions from the Baltic to the Adriatic with an army of 400,000 men, subsidised by the British at the rate of £5 million a year. Uncertainty, however, remained over the intentions of Prussia; and in October the Tsar travelled to Berlin in the hope of inducing his friend, King Frederick William III of Prussia, to enter the campaign. But, although the King was well-disposed towards the Tsar, he cautiously refused to commit himself until he had seen in whose favour the war was going. And by the time the Tsar left Berlin for the Austro-Russian headquarters on 5 November, the prospect of the Allies was already beginning to look bleak.

At the end of the third week in October the Austrian commander, General Mack, suffered a shattering humiliation. Cut off by the swiftly moving French divisions of Murat and Soult and faced with

Marche précipitée de L'armée Russe Volant au secours des prussiens.

mutinous threats from his own senior officers, Mack was forced to surrender at Ulm, thus taking out of action more than thirty thousand of Austria's most experienced troops. Mack had made a double miscalculation: he thought it impossible for Napoleon to concentrate a formidable army on the Danube so rapidly; and he also expected a Russian force to have reached Bavaria by the middle of October. The slow response of the Russians led to early recriminations between the two principal Allied Powers.

Before leaving St Petersburg for Berlin, Alexander had appointed Kutuzov, as Russia's most experienced general, to command the expeditionary force in southern Germany. But Kutuzov needed far longer to concentrate his army than Alexander or the Austrians had anticipated. Kutuzov did not reach the Austrian frontier in Galicia until 22 September, ten days later than planned, and he brought with him only a vanguard of 38,000 men. It took the Russians another three weeks to cover two hundred and fifty miles across Moravia and take up positions at the confluence of the rivers Danube and Inn. It was there, on 23 October, that Kutuzov heard the bad news from Ulm. He immediately decided to retreat down the Danube towards Vienna, conducting a series of holding operations so as to delay the French until he had made contact with the principal Russian army, which was still moving slowly westwards into Moravia. Kutuzov's strategic plan was sound: it was based upon the traditional theories of Rumyantsev and, in many respects, it anticipated the successful dispositions of 1812. The French were to

'Precipitate march of the flying Russian army to help the Prussians'. A French cartoon of the Napoleonic wars, 1806.

be lured eastwards and denied a set-piece battle: their lines of communication would thus be dangerously extended in wretched wintry conditions; and they would be exposed to a threat from the Prussians in the north and the Austrian army of the Archduke Charles in the south. Time and distance were on Russia's side; and at all costs Napoleon must be prevented from gaining a rapid victory by a decisive encounter of the main armies fought prematurely. Napoleon, of course, was fully aware of his danger, with the finest troops in the Grand Army four hundred miles from his own natural frontier. As soon as he had entered Vienna (which he was able to do, with little resistance, on 13 November) he began to make separate approaches to the Austrian and Russian rulers, hoping at the very least to increase the suspicion between them.

Kutuzov's retreat from the Inn to Moravia was marked by a succession of sharp actions at Lambach, Amstetten, Melk and Krems and by the very real danger that he would himself suffer a fate similar to Mack's; for, with the fall of Vienna, Murat and Soult were able to turn northwards, threatening to cut off the tired Russian columns as they fell back on Znaim. Murat was checked by two events: an insincere offer by Kutuzov of an armistice (which gave him time to complete his dispositions); and a brilliant delaying action fought by Bagration between the villages of Hollabrunn and Schöngraben, twenty-five miles north-west of Vienna. All these episodes are poignantly described by Tolstoy at the end of Book II of *War and Peace*: he based his narrative on a semi-official Russian account by Mikhailovsky-Danilevsky and on Thiers' superb *History of the Consulate and Empire*; and there are few sections of the novel which correspond so closely to the accepted chronicle of events. But, since Tolstoy was primarily concerned with the reaction of private individuals to the known facts of history, he did not emphasise the extent to which this grim confrontation of French and Russian infantry on 16 November saved the bulk of Kutuzov's men. Three days later Kutuzov made contact with the main Russian army at Wischau, where he was soon afterwards joined by the survivors from Bagration's division, reduced to half-strength after its courageous delaying action. By 22 November a Russo-Austrian army of 87,000 men was massed in central Moravia, and Tsar Alexander, together with the ruler of Austria, Emperor Francis, had set up headquarters in the city of Olmütz (known nowadays by its Czech name, Olomouc). Napoleon and the force which he had recently baptised *La Grande Armée* were forty-five miles away, in the Moravian capital of Brünn (now Brno).

On paper the Allies held every advantage. They had in all, at that moment, nearly 30,000 more men than the French, with considerable superiority in cavalry and artillery. Another Russian army was concentrating in Poland, although with customary slowness; and there was a small Austrian army on Napoleon's left flank in

The Approach to Austerlitz

Bohemia, away to the north. Even if Prussia continued to hesitate, it was clear that the position of the Grand Army was becoming more and more precarious. Yet Kutuzov still wished to avoid battle and maintain the retreat. His troops were living off the land – no easy task in mid-winter – and he proposed that as soon as they had absorbed such food as central Moravia could offer, they should retire eastward again, leaving a barren area for Napoleon to occupy, if he so desired. Winter and hunger might thus become Russia's ally rather than her adversary.

Few at headquarters heeded his advice. Emperor Francis and his officers disliked the idea of abandoning tracts of their homeland, their estates and their towns and villages. Nor did Tsar Alexander show any patience with Kutuzov. He was more impressed by the

views of an Austrian staff officer, Weyrother, who spoke convincingly
of the local terrain. Bagration and some of the other senior Russian
commanders had met Weyrother before; in 1799 he had presented
himself to Suvorov as an expert on the geography of the Swiss Alps
and had then shown the Marshal, on the map, a route from Altdorf
to Schwyz which did not exist, and indeed could not exist as there
was a sheer wall of mountain in the way. But the Tsar would hear
no criticisms of Weyrother; and when the Austrian proposed an
enveloping movement to cut off Napoleon from Vienna and drive
him against the Army of Bohemia, Alexander welcomed the plan
as though it were the product of inspired revelation rather than a
variant on the time-hallowed strategy of Hannibal at Cannae, as it
was. On Wednesday, 27 November, the Allies began to move forward confidently towards Brünn and the road to the south; by the
following Tuesday they were a broken army, and the Tsar was in
headlong flight to the east.

Napoleon had hoped, for more than a week, that the Allies would
turn and offer him a decisive engagement; but he never anticipated
a full counter-offensive so soon after the completion of Kutuzov's
retreat. It was, however, easy enough to read Alexander's intentions,
and the French watched with satisfaction the awkward crablike
manoeuvre by which the Allies sought to move their columns south

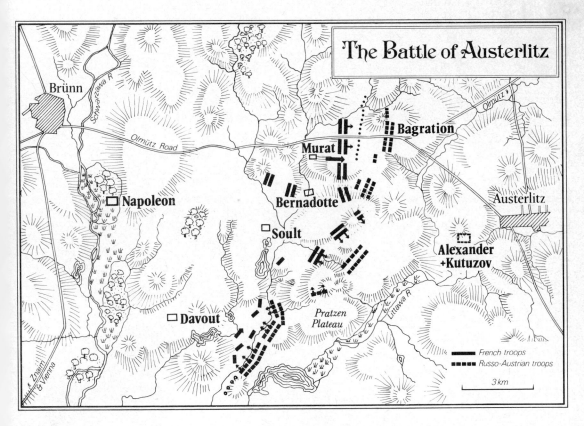

of the Olmütz-Brünn road. For the moment, Napoleon was prepared to feign a reluctance for battle: this was partly because he
wished to lure his enemy into an unfavourable position, but it was
also because he was awaiting another 16,000 men, part of Bernadotte's First Corps hurrying up from Znaim and Davout's Third
Corps from Vienna. They were not expected to reach the Brünn
area until dusk on Sunday, 1 December. Soon after noon that Sunday Napoleon ordered the evacuation of the plateau of Pratzen, a
commanding position four miles to the west of Austerlitz (Slavkov),
which was then a small village around the chateau of the Kaunitz
family. The Tsar could hardly believe that the French would leave
so valuable a defensive obstacle unoccupied, and he immediately
determined to take advantage of what he assumed was an elementary
mistake. That evening he halted the Allied movement southwards
and ordered the line to wheel westwards, a manoeuvre which caused
considerable confusion, especially to the Austrian vanguard, who
found themselves floundering in slippery mud on the edge of the
plateau. Weyrother conveyed to the Russian and Austrian generals
the Tsar's intention of launching a general attack on the French position in the morning. Kutuzov accepted his master's decision, an act
of loyal obedience which Alexander, in later years, found it hard to
forgive him.

The weather, which had been bitterly cold, turned milder over
the week-end and there was a thaw during Sunday. It was not sufficient to break the ice on the lakes and ponds but it made the marshy
meadows between the plateau and Austerlitz extremely treacherous.
The change in temperature also meant that the countryside was
covered in fog on the Monday morning until about eight o'clock.
To Napoleon's elation, 'the sun of Austerlitz' then broke through,
so that from his position of vantage on high ground to the north-
west of the plateau he could see Russian and Austrian columns
moving steadily into the mists which still clung to the valleys below
Pratzen. He waited until half-past eight before authorising Marshal
Soult, who was at his side, to attack the weakened Russian centre,
sending the cavalry down on to the plateau from high ground in the
north, thereby taking the Russians on their right flank. It was almost
precisely at this moment when Napoleon released Soult that the
Tsar was upbraiding Kutuzov for his hesitancy in pressing forward
across the plateau (a scene faithfully recorded by Tolstoy from
contemporary recollections).

The Russian line broke under the unexpected impact but was
hastily reformed; and it seemed, momentarily, as if the fighting
might swing in favour of the Allies, who in this particular part of the
battlefield outnumbered the French by some three thousand men.
But a second cavalry brigade completed the rout, sweeping the
Russians back off the plateau. The French had thus bisected their
enemies at the pivotal point of their abortive attack. The Russians

Prince Andrew Bolkonsky
at the battle of
Austerlitz. An illustration
to *War and Peace* by
Dementy Shmarinov.

were not yet beaten, but all co-ordination between the Allies seemed to have ended with this shattering blow on the plateau. The Russian Guard cavalry disputed the eastern edge of the plateau around the middle of the morning; and farther north Bagration attempted to turn the left flank of the French, only to find himself heavily engaged with Murat's light cavalry. There was a lull on the plateau between eleven o'clock in the morning and one o'clock in the afternoon, for Napoleon did not want to make a similar mistake to the Russians, advancing impetuously without being sure of what was happening in the northern part of the battlefield. But in the early afternoon the Grand Army moved resolutely forward, driving what was left of the Russians back through Austerlitz itself and down the valley of the Littawa towards the Carpathians and the distant safety of the Hungarian plain. It began to snow and an early dusk brought respite to the Russians. Kutuzov was wounded and the Tsar pitifully ill with a fever of remorse. The Allies, in six hours fighting, had lost 27,000 men, more than three times as many as the French.

The battle of Austerlitz determined the outcome of the campaign, as Napoleon had anticipated. In later years he declared it was the easiest and most decisive of all his victories. Emperor Francis asked for a truce, and within four weeks the Austrians had signed the Peace of Pressburg, by which they accepted exclusion from Italy, Dalmatia and southern Germany. The Prussians, while congratulating themselves on their good sense in staying out of the war, hurriedly reached an understanding with France. Tsar Alexander meanwhile withdrew the battered remnant of his army across the Austro-Russian frontier but did not formally conclude peace with Napoleon. Operations continued throughout 1806 in the southern Adriatic, where a Russian naval force, supported by 13,000 men, established itself in Corfu and on the islands of Vis and Korcula, rousing the Montenegrins to attack a French garrison in Dubrovnik. Yet, although this isolated side-show irritated the new Charlemagne in Paris, it was never of major importance to him; and he was able to concentrate on restoring the French economy and re-drawing the map of Germany without any serious threat from the Russians.

Alexander returned to St Petersburg sick at heart. Russia had suffered her greatest defeat since the battle of Narva in November 1700. Yet, strangely enough, his people welcomed their Tsar as though he were a military conqueror. It was late at night when he reached his capital but thousands gathered outside the Winter Palace, braving the bitter cold in order to cheer him. They happily explained Austerlitz away: it was, they said, all a consequence of Austria's ineptitude and Prussia's reluctance to honour her obligations; and there were some – as Tolstoy records – who took the strangely detached view that no one could expect to win victories year after year and that it was time for Russia's luck to turn against her, anyhow. More sophisticated observers were less complacent.

The campaign had shown both the old-fashioned character of Russian training and the folly of permitting a young and inexperienced sovereign to over-ride the strategy of his field commanders. The Tsar's own family did not spare his feelings and he was especially criticised by his younger brother, Grand Duke Constantine, who had commanded the reserve at Austerlitz and who held Bagration in particular esteem. So, indeed, did almost everybody else, for Bagration was the only Russian general whose reputation had been enhanced by the seven-week campaign.

But the effects of Austerlitz were not confined to the three empires whose armies clashed on that December day. The French successes profoundly impressed Russia's southern neighbour, Turkey, hitherto hostile to the man who had brought Europe's war to the Levant; and in 1806 Napoleon and his foreign minister, Talleyrand, began a diplomatic offensive which threatened to deprive the Russian Empire of its most cherished conquests. 'The ultimate object of my policy,' wrote Napoleon to Talleyrand in June 1806, 'is to make a triple alliance of myself, the Porte (i.e. Turkey) and Persia, aimed against Russia, directly or by implication.' The bait to tempt the Sultan was a suggestion that a successful Franco-Turkish combination against the Tsar could lead to the recovery of the Crimea and the elimination of Russia as a Black Sea Power. There was no need for the French to encourage the Persians, for they were at war with the Russian 'Army of the Caucasus' throughout Alexander's reign, and indeed for long afterwards.

The Russians speedily became aware of the renewed interest of Napoleon in the Eastern Question; but they responded to the French activities at Constantinople with a mixture of alarm and satisfaction; for at least the military party in St Petersburg now had an excuse to resume operations against the traditional enemy, Turkey, rather than risk another conflict with the Grand Army on the Central European plains. It was resolved, in the spring of 1806, that should there be any outward sign of French support for Turkey, the Russians would immediately advance southwards and, as a preventative measure, occupy the Danubian provinces of Moldavia and Wallachia (nowadays the core of Roumania, but then forming part of Turkey's north-western frontier). A considerable Russian army was concentrated in the Ukraine throughout the summer of 1806, and it duly entered the Principalities in the last week of November. The Turks, in reply, formally declared war on Russia before the end of the year. A conflict thus began which was to continue until the spring of 1812, proving itself to be a constant distraction from the greater menace which was building up against Russia in the West.

Meanwhile, Napoleon's army had been forced, against his will, to resume its march into Germany. The Prussians, having missed the opportunity to intervene effectively in the previous autumn, became

General Rapp surrenders the Austrian standard to Napoleon at Austerlitz.

alarmed at the creation of Napoleon's puppet states within Germany and were belatedly conscious of their own political eclipse. In July 1806 King Frederick William III concluded a new military alliance with Tsar Alexander, with whom he remained on terms of close personal friendship (to the fury of the other members of the Russian Imperial family). In the last week of September, without prior consultation of the Russians, Frederick William sent an ultimatum to Napoleon insisting on an immediate withdrawal of the French from all German lands east of the Rhine. This was a colossal error of judgement on the part of the Prussian King. Napoleon marched into Prussia on 7 October and a week later, before the Russians could put an army into the field, scattered the Prussian soldiery in the twin battles of Jena and Auerstadt. By the time a Russian army reached East Prussia, Napoleon was installed in Berlin; and the French could claim, within twenty days of fighting, the capture of 140,000 Prussian prisoners-of-war and eight hundred field guns. Frederick William III fled to Memel and sought Russian protection. With him was his consort, Queen Louise, a woman of remarkable charm and personality, towards whom the Tsar felt a strong romantic attachment.

137

The collapse of the Prussian State posed a new problem for Alexander and his advisers. The third Partition of Poland in 1795 had made Warsaw a Prussian possession and the French accordingly made an unopposed entry into the former Polish capital on 27 November. A large group of the Polish nobility and bourgeoisie favoured the French, believing that Napoleon would restore their nation; and a Polish Legion had already been formed to fight within the Grand Army. As yet Napoleon was not prepared to identify himself with Polish national aspirations, partly because the intricacies of the Polish Question were unfamiliar to him and he had not expected to be confronted with them so soon. But in St Petersburg it was assumed that the French would immediately take up the Polish cause, thereby inciting the Russian Poles to rise against their masters. So serious a political threat prompted the Tsar to seek the aid of Holy Russia against the Revolution of the Godless; and a solemn anathema was read in every Orthodox Church within the Empire stigmatising Napoleon as 'the principal enemy of mankind, one who worships idols and whores . . . and, surpassing all his other dreadful crimes in wickedness, intends to have himself proclaimed the Messiah.' If it was hoped these stirring words would awaken the Russian masses to the peril at their gates, they failed in their purpose. The new campaign was not greeted with the excitement of 1805. Half the nobility thought it was being fought for the sake of Prussia; the remainder appear to have been convinced its purpose was to Russianise the Prussian Poles. Understandably, neither cause was popular.

On this occasion, Alexander entrusted the active command to a general whose name was not associated with the events of the previous year, Count Levin Bennigsen. On 26 December he withstood a determined French assault on his positions at Pultusk, but the weather was so bad that Napoleon decided to call off the campaigning until the spring, establishing himself in central Poland. Bennigsen, for his part, had no intention of relaxing the pressure and at the end of January he made a tentative probe towards the garrison city of Thorn, but he was forced back into East Prussia. On 8 February 1807 he took up defensive positions around the town of Eylau, in a very treacherous terrain where there were numerous small lakes frozen beneath three or four feet of snow. The fighting was even bloodier than Austerlitz, nearly fifty thousand men falling during the day. Much of the battle took place in a blinding blizzard and all of it was fought out in appalling visibility. Both sides subsequently claimed a victory, but since Napoleon was left master of the field while Bennigsen fell back on Königsberg, the battle ended in favour of the French. Yet no one could regard Eylau as a triumph of arms; and for Napoleon the indecisive slaughter was a terrible warning against waging a winter campaign on the Eastern fringes of the continent.

Napoleon receiving the Queen of Prussia at Tilsit, Tsar Alexander hovering behind.

There followed three and a half months of doubt and manoeuvre, in which it seemed as if neither side wished to resume the war but each suspected the other of deception. Napoleon spent some of these weeks trying to rule his Empire from the wretched discomfort of field headquarters in the small town of Osterode, south-west of the Masurian Lakes; and on 1 April he moved to the castle at Finkenstein, which was almost as comfortless and twice as grim. For much of the spring the Tsar and the King of Prussia were less than sixty miles away from him, at Bartenstein, another relic from Europe's medieval frontier. The campaign might well have ended without another major battle, for Alexander was seriously considering an approach to the French: he knew the war was unpopular within his empire; and he was becoming increasingly aware that his British ally was not in accord with his ambitions, frowning on his designs against Turkey and refusing to open a Second Front by landing British troops on the mainland of the continent. Moreover, the subsidy guaranteed by the government in London seemed pitiably small in comparison with Russia's great sacrifices and it was unfortunate that ambassadorial discussion on political and strategic questions should so often have ended in British requests for more privileges for London merchants. Better, perhaps, an understanding with the Antichrist than renewed sacrifices to the Moloch in Westminster.

But before serious negotiations could begin, Bennigsen stumbled into battle. Early in June, hoping to gain a better tactical position for the defence of Königsberg, Bennigsen made a thrust on Ney's principal base of operations, fifty miles south of the city. For over a week there was intermittent fighting along the banks of the river Alle, covering Königsberg. The Alle is a steep-banked stream running between broken, wooded country for more than forty miles; it is too deep for fords and there were only some half a dozen bridges along this section of the river. One of these was at the town of Friedland, which Bennigsen reached late at night on 13 June. He immediately ordered three pontoon bridges to be thrown across the river and poured an army of 60,000 men into Friedland itself, on the west bank. At dawn he launched a surprise attack on the French reserve corps under Marshal Lannes, who had been marching parallel to him for some days.

At first there was nothing to suggest that the skirmishing on 14 June at Friedland marked the beginning of a great battle. Bennigsen's men were tired and hungry from night marches and only Bagration's cavalry on the left flank still showed stout morale. On the other hand, when the action began Napoleon and the main French army were eighteen miles away, by a coincidence on the old battlefield of Eylau. Lannes, though outnumbered two to one, checked Bennigsen's initial attack; and the Russians withdrew into an ill-considered defensive position, in a bend of the river, with a small tributary separating their two flanks and only the Alle behind

The Treaty of Tilsit, 1807; Napoleon meets Alexander in the middle of the river Niemen after the rout of the Russians at Friedland.

them. Concentric hills looked down on Friedland itself and on the
Russian defences. When Napoleon arrived during the afternoon, he
ordered an attack at the earliest opportunity. Ney's cavalry swept
forward at five o'clock and the French artillery destroyed the pontoon bridge and raked Bagration's infantry with continuous canister
fire for almost half an hour, killing some four thousand men. By
seven in the evening what was left of the town of Friedland was in
French hands; and by ten o'clock the principal Russian army in the
battle zone was destroyed, only some five thousand men falling back
with Bennigsen along the west bank of the Alle.

Five days later envoys from the Tsar sought a truce, and an armistice was concluded on 21 June. Both Napoleon and Alexander
needed peace: Napoleon because he had already spent too long away
from the centre of his empire and dared not improvise an invasion
of Russia; and Alexander, because he had lost confidence in his

generals and in his allies, convincing himself that he hated the English at least as much as he did his French adversary. The two emperors met at Tilsit on 25 June 1807 to discuss, not merely a settlement of the disputes between them, but the conclusion of a Franco-Russian alliance.

Tolstoy says virtually nothing in *War and Peace* of the dismal campaigns of Eylau and Friedland. But the irony of the Tilsit meeting was a fillip to his pen, and his narrative well catches the absurd pretence at friendship between recent enemies in the little town beside the Niemen. He describes, with careful attention to historical detail, the embarrassment caused by Napoleon's insistence on decorating a Russian soldier with the Legion of Honour; but, as so often in Tolstoy's novels, it is a small fictitious incident which best preserves the atmosphere of the time:

On the 13th of June the French and Russian Emperors arrived in Tilsit. Boris Drubetskoy had asked the important personage on whom he was in attendance to include him in the suite appointed for the stay at Tilsit.

'I should like to see the great man,' he said, alluding to Napoleon, whom hitherto he, like everyone else, had always called Buonaparte.

'You are speaking of Buonaparte?' asked the general, smiling. Boris looked at the general inquiringly and immediately saw that he was being tested.

'I am speaking, Prince, of the Emperor Napoleon,' he replied. The general patted him on the shoulder with a smile.

'You will go far,' he said, and took him to Tilsit with him.

No contemporary record exists to show precisely what each Emperor said to the other, nor is it possible to assess the sincerity of their mutual magnanimity. The terms of the treaties concluded on 7 July and 9 July speak for themselves: although the Russians renounced their rights in the Mediterranean, no part of the Russian Empire was surrendered to Napoleon (indeed, Alexander even gained the province of Bialystok, formerly in Prussian Poland); Prussia, at Alexander's personal intercession, was allowed to survive as a nominally sovereign state east of the Elbe; and a Grand Duchy of Warsaw was established, technically under the King of Saxony and in practice administered by French nominees. Secret agreements pledged Alexander to assist Napoleon in his economic warfare against Britain, by excluding English goods from Russia and cutting off all trade with British ports. The Tsar was to have a free hand to pick a quarrel with Sweden and annex Finland, if he wished; and there would also be collaboration between the French and the Russians over the affairs of Turkey, provided that Alexander did not seek to establish a Russian presence in Constantinople itself, a city which Napoleon insisted was 'the centre of world empire'. After the triple defeats of Austerlitz, Eylau and Friedland these were remarkably generous terms for Russia.

Alexander encouraged his family to believe he had successfully

An English cartoon showing Alexander I and Napoleon at Tilsit, in 1807, embracing on the raft where their negotiations took place, while the King of Prussia tries to rescue his crown.

duped Napoleon, winning a free hand in Scandinavia and the eastern Balkans by acknowledging French hegemony in central and western Europe. He even maintained to his critics in St Petersburg that he had gained recognition of his own claim to be treated as an equal arbiter in Europe's affairs. Perhaps he really believed it. But Napoleon, too, was satisfied. He needed a lasting truce on the continent: it was essential for him to consolidate his position, not only in Germany, but at home in France as well. Whatever Alexander might feel, Napoleon was convinced Russia had now fallen into position within his new European order, a junior partner in a flourishing concern. Should Russia not be content to remain a subordinate, then he would have to march eastwards across the Niemen; but this was an enterprise that required long preparation. Tilsit would at least slow down the pace of events; he reckoned his meeting with the Tsar to have been a dazzling triumph of diplomacy.

6 The Inevitable Conflict

Although the campaigns of 1806 and 1807 had never fired any enthusiasm among the Tsar's subjects, there were few people in Moscow or St Petersburg ready to champion the merits of the Tilsit peace. It was humiliating to have to honour as Emperor of the French a person condemned from every pulpit as 'the enemy of mankind' less than eight months previously; and there remained in both cities an influential group of exiles from Prussia (and from France itself) who continued to stir up resistance to Napoleon's policy. Moreover, most sections of the population had real grievances of their own: for there was chronic financial chaos in the three years which followed the Tilsit settlement, and the rouble fell to less than a fifth of its nominal value. Since the Tsar had undertaken to adhere to the Continental System (the Napoleonic blockade of Britain), Russia's foreign trade was more than halved and the Baltic ports, including St Petersburg itself, suffered grievously. The bigger landowners, as well as the merchants, were hard hit; for the prohibition of timber, flax and hemp exports to England threatened ruin on many of the larger estates. Members of the nobility and gentry with estates in the western lands were also worried by the revival of Polish national feeling across the frontier, especially as the new Grand Duchy of Warsaw could lean for support on the military might of the Napoleonic armies.

Tsar Alexander was determined to gain what he could from French goodwill as rapidly as possible. In February 1808 the Russians marched into Finland, which was then a Swedish possession, and within three months the whole of the Finnish peninsula was in Russian hands. The Swedes, however, held out for more than a year and maintained serious guerrilla activity against Russian supply lines across the peninsula before accepting the loss of Finland in September 1809. Although the Tsar and his ministers sought to mobilise patriotic feeling by representing the campaign as the completion of Peter the Great's policy, the war with Sweden was far from popular. It completed the ruin of Baltic trade and, even if it improved the security of St Petersburg from outside attack, society in both Russian capitals tended to condemn the campaign as a waste of men and material. The renewal of operations against the Turks in the spring of 1809 was more readily accepted, though here, too, there was a feeling that the Tsar should conserve his army and its munitions for the next round of the contest in Europe.

Previous page Alexander I presents the Cossacks to Napoleon, July 1807.

This was indeed what, to a large extent, Alexander believed he was doing. While outwardly lauding Napoleon, he was conscious of public hostility, and he began slowly to prepare for a resumption of the great duel between the two empires. In September 1808 he sent a letter to his mother, who had no sympathy with her son's policy of appeasement: Russia, he claimed, 'needs to breathe freely for a time and, during this valuable interlude, must build up our material and our forces. . . . Only in the deepest silence must we work and not by making our armaments or our preparations known, nor by loud denunciations of the one whom we are defying.'

It must, however, be admitted that Alexander's policy was remarkably devious; for in that same month he travelled to Erfurt in central Germany and appeared to enjoy being fêted by Napoleon, who flattered his guest by excessive attention to the details of hospitality. The best actors and actresses in Paris were fetched to Erfurt so as to entertain the Tsar and the German Princes. Alexander was provided with enchanting dancing partners at the balls which enlivened the autumn evenings; and – with a shade less tact – he was invited to tour the battlefield of Jena, where his host explained precisely how he had defeated Alexander's Prussian ally almost exactly two years previously. Socially, Erfurt was a sensational gathering of the new European elite: politically it was less remarkable. Napoleon confirmed his willingness to see Finland and the Danubian principalities incorporated in Russia; and Alexander gave a verbal undertaking to assist Napoleon should France find herself at war with Austria. Privately the Tsar was put on his guard against Napoleon's overweening ambition by conversations he held with Talleyrand, who had been French Foreign Minister until the previous year and was still his Emperor's chief adviser on European affairs.

The breach between the Tilsit allies became openly apparent in the following year. Alexander complained that the French had never withdrawn their garrisons from Prussia, as Napoleon had promised; and in Paris there was bitter recrimination against the Russians for conniving at smuggling on a grand scale, so that some merchants were even trading with England. More serious still was the effect of the brief Franco-Austrian War of 1809: for while Napoleon was inflicting another defeat on Emperor Francis at Wagram, the Tsar mobilised with reluctance and ordered his troops to move forward into Galicia with such circumspection that they eventually suffered only two casualties. Napoleon, irritated by the Russian response, ceased to trouble himself over Alexander's susceptibilities: he

Napoleon in his marriage robes. His choice of bride, rejecting Alexander's sister, did much to exacerbate the growing dissension between the two Emperors.

extended the Grand Duchy of Warsaw with territory annexed from Austria and, at the same time, he refused to give the Tsar any assurance that he would not further enlarge the Grand Duchy or use the name 'Poland' to describe his puppet creation. Relations between Paris and St Petersburg were strained but not broken; and in the closing months of 1809 it seemed likely that Napoleon might take Alexander's youngest sister, Anna Pavlovna, as his second wife. But in March 1810 Napoleon married the Habsburg Archduchess, Marie Louise (who, at eighteen, was three years older than Anna). Alexander was doubly vexed: he resented the presumption of a Bonaparte in having considered marriage with a member of the Russian Royal House in the first place; and he resented even more Napoleon's choice of a Habsburg bride, rather than a Romanov, in the end.

To Alexander the Austrian marriage seemed proof that French policy had again changed and Emperor Francis and his foreign minister, Metternich, were now Napoleon's alliance partners. This was a considerable oversimplification of both Austrian and French diplomatic objectives; but there was certainly no occasion after February 1810 when Napoleon offered the Russians any concessions of substance. The Tsar for his part began to patronise the Russo-Polish nobility, a direct challenge to the French-sponsored Grand Duchy and a move interpreted by Napoleon as reckless meddling. Relations between the two empires deteriorated even more rapidly at the end of the year when Alexander formally took Russia out of the Continental System, throwing the ports of the Empire open to British trade and imposing a defiant tariff on French luxury goods. A fortnight later Napoleon annexed the German duchy of Oldenburg, whose ruler was the Tsar's uncle and whose heir had married the Tsar's favourite sister, Catherine. 'It seems that blood must flow again,' wrote Alexander with resignation, as the Oldenburg crisis came to a head; and he gave orders that neither the arms works in Tula nor the ordnance centre at Alexandrovsk should miss a day's work that year by observing the holidays of Epiphany and Easter. A new tone of stubborn determination had come into the Tsar's public pronouncements.

At the start of Book IX of *War and Peace*, and in the second Epilogue, Tolstoy emphasises his own belief in the inevitability of a historical process; and he pours scorn on those writers who searched for the origins of the 1812 campaign in human follies or decisions – the ambition of the French, the resolution of the Tsar, 'the mistakes of diplomats, and so on'. This determinist philosophy was mainly the product of a later generation's experience and reflection; and yet, strangely enough, both Alexander and Napoleon shared at times a similar fatalism, a recognition that inexorable forces were moulding historical events and that they themselves only partially controlled

Marie-Louise of Austria, daughter of Francis I and bride of Napoleon, in her wedding robes.

what was to happen. To Napoleon this force was 'Destiny', whose child he consistently believed himself to be; while Alexander genuinely saw himself as a vehicle intended to fulfill the purpose of God. By the spring of 1811 each ruler had convinced himself that 'Fate' demanded a renewed conflict between their two empires, that they could not co-exist in amity; but each also thought it was his responsibility to determine when war should come and where the contest should be fought out; and hence they claimed an assertion of will and a primacy of personality which Tolstoy would have denied them.

The Tsar seriously considered ordering a surprise attack on the French in the spring of 1811. He moved several regiments westwards from Bessarabia; but, on reflection, he saw that the preventative wars launched by Prussia in 1806 and Austria in 1809 had proved disastrous; and, abandoning the project, he concentrated on improving Russia's defences. Napoleon had other problems in 1811: the persistent struggle in Spain and Portugal; an economic crisis within France; and even the unfamiliar difficulties of unemployment. But on 16 August he gave instructions for work to begin on the planning of a new Russian campaign. It was to involve units from all the territories of the French Empire and detachments from his allies; and it was to be planned with a meticulous detail given to no previous enterprise, for it was essential that he should be able to put a massive army into the field and to maintain it as he advanced into the endless Russian plains. His staff were given ten months to complete their plans.

The Russians were well-informed of Napoleon's intentions. Until his discovery in February 1812 they had a spy in the Department of War Administration in Paris who was able to send them details of troop movements; and thereafter they obtained further information from Berlin and from Vienna. In the third week of April 1812 Alexander left St Petersburg and took up residence at Vilna, some seventy miles from the frontier with Prussia, where the Grand Army had its easternmost line of outposts. Napoleon and Marie Louise set out from Paris on 9 May and on the evening of 16 May arrived in Dresden, where the Emperor of the French had summoned all the German rulers, together with his father-in-law (Emperor Francis) and Metternich. For twelve days he lingered in Dresden, ostentatiously enjoying the pageant of imperial authority while emphasising to his brother sovereigns and their vassals the magnitude of the task before him. Then on 29 May he set out from Dresden for the Vistula, where the Grand Army had been concentrating during the previous four weeks. Some had come from Italy and from Dalmatia, others (including some battalions of the famous Imperial Guard) had been brought from Spain, a march of seventeen hundred miles. Most assumed that it would be a brief campaign, with an early battle deciding the issue.

The Approach to Borodino

By mid-June more than 400,000 men were deployed along the river Vistula between Danzig and Warsaw, ready to move forward into East Prussia and take up their war stations on the banks of the Niemen, which formed the frontier with Russia. This formidable force was supported by more than 1100 guns and some 80,000 cavalry horses, together with engineer units and other auxiliary troops. Only a third of the Grand Army came from metropolitan France; for, although the army was commanded by the great Marshals of the Empire (Ney, Murat, Davout, Berthier, Oudinot), it was a remarkably cosmopolitan force containing Italians, Swiss, Poles, Danes, Dutch, Croats, Saxons, Mecklenburgers, Hamburgers, Württembergers, Holsteiners, Bavarians, Rhinelanders, Portuguese and Spaniards. On the southern flank was an Austrian Army Corps, 30,000 men under Prince Schwarzenberg; and in the north a Prussian corps, some 20,000 strong. Morale varied: neither the Austrians nor the Prussians liked the war; and there were other units who had every intention of deserting at the earliest opportunity. But the spirit of the veteran regiments was unbroken; and the so-called 'Young Guard' were eager to win distinction in battle.

The Grand Army was faced by the Russian 'Army of the West' which was divided into three groups: Barclay de Tolly, as Minister of War, commanded the First Army (118,000 men) facing Napoleon along the Niemen; Bagration commanded the Second Army (35,000 men) to the south of Vilna; and General Tormassov commanded the small Third Army which faced Schwarzenberg's Austrians in the most southerly sector. A further reserve force was on its way from the Turkish Front, where operations had ceased earlier in the year. To his generals' consternation, the Tsar insisted that the threat to his empire was so grave that he must personally assume the responsibilities of command. Once again he had, unfortunately, discovered a foreign military genius, General Ernst von Pfuel, a Prussian specialist in the military history of classical Rome; and the Tsar preferred Pfuel's advice to that of his own commanders. Pfuel believed in withdrawing the main Russian force to an entrenched camp at Drissa, leaving Bagration to attack the French as they laid siege to Drissa. Neither the Russians nor the other foreign officers in the Tsar's service liked the plan, not least because they doubted if the Drissa defences could withstand an assault long enough for Bagration to make contact with the enemy. Throughout June, discussions over the best defensive strategy continued around the council tables in Vilna, without any final decision being taken. On the night of 24 June the Tsar, his aides and his generals went to a grand ball at Zakret, a few miles outside Vilna, where General Bennigsen had an estate. It was there that Alexander received news that Napoleon's

This standard of the 140th Infantry regiment of Napoleon's army was captured by Russian troops at Borodino.

troops had crossed the Niemen early that morning: the invasion of Russia had begun at last.

There was never any formal declaration of war, only a proclamation read to the invading army and putting the blame for 'the Second Polish War' on the perfidy of the Russians. Virtually no resistance awaited the first troops and by the afternoon more than 160,000 men had crossed the three pontoon bridges thrown over the Niemen. The city of Kaunas fell immediately into French hands; and the second and third waves of the Grand Army came over the same bridges without even seeing the enemy. Within four days the first columns were approaching Vilna itself and by 30 June Napoleon had established his headquarters in Russia's third largest city. Its inhabitants told him that the Tsar had left, heading eastwards with his staff two days previously; but there were no troops left to defend Vilna against the invader, and no sign of the early battle which Napoleon had anticipated. He found it extremely perplexing that the Russians should have refused to put up a fight for such a prize. The possibility that they were not in earnest over the campaign occurred to him, and he was therefore reluctant to take any political move which would make peace harder to obtain. Hence he declined to appeal to the Russian peasantry by proclaiming serf-emancipation; and he refused to unite Vilna with Warsaw and Cracow in a Polish State.

Not for the last time in the campaign, Napoleon's irritability was increased by the unpredictable weather. None of his staff officers had allowed for difficult climatic conditions during the summer months, and yet along the route from Kaunas the sun had taken a heavy toll of the horses, and the heat was so intense that veterans were reminded of the Egyptian Expedition. Now, in Vilna itself and the surrounding countryside, it rained as heavily as in a tropical monsoon and the cavalry of Davout and Murat could make no contact with the retreating enemy down the mud-caked roads.

It was heavy going, too, for Alexander. He had left Vilna intending to fall back on Drissa, where he would await the arrival of Barclay's First Army, while Bagration was withdrawing through Minsk so as to have room for manoeuvre should Napoleon strike north-east-wards towards the new capital rather than against Smolensk and Moscow. The Tsar did not reach Drissa until 8 July, but even so he was two days ahead of Barclay. It did not take the Russian commanders long to see that, as they had feared, the hastily erected earthworks around Drissa would not afford adequate protection from the Grand Army. Colonel von Clausewitz, who was later to become the most distinguished of all military writers, was one of the Prussian émigrés then serving under Barclay's command; and he was horrified by the Drissa camp: 'If the Russians had not abandoned this position of their own accord,' he later declared, 'they would have been attacked from the rear . . . and forced to surrender.' Gradually Barclay convinced Alexander of the need to move closer to the main road to Moscow, if only to make contact with Bagration, who was nearly two hundred miles to the south of Drissa. On 15 July Barclay's men, with the Tsar's personal bodyguard, began to move slowly southwards, leaving Wittgenstein to protect the route to St Petersburg with a force of 25,000 experienced troops.

Inducing the Tsar to leave Drissa was, however, only one aspect of a much bigger problem for the army command. All the senior officers wanted Alexander back in his capital, partly because they were apprehensive that he would discover yet another paper theorist to succeed Pfuel, but also because they genuinely thought he could rally public opinion in Moscow and St Petersburg, which was still lukewarm in support of the war. At Polotsk General Arakcheev and two other close advisers of the Tsar urged him to leave the army and resume his responsibilities at the centre of affairs. Reluctantly he accepted their advice and set out for Moscow on 16 July, arriving there seven days later and receiving an enthusiastically loyal greeting from the people of the old capital. On Monday, 27 July, Alexander was given pledges of support from separate assemblies of the merchants and the nobility (a scene which Tolstoy makes the climax of the closing chapters in Book IX). There is no doubt that as long as the Tsar was seen to be resolutely defying Napoleon, he could count on the support of his peoples; and for purposes of morale it was better for him to be with them rather than in the field of battle.

On that same Monday Napoleon believed he was at last about to force Barclay's First Army into action. For nearly a month he had waited for news of its position, constantly denied the early engagement he so desired. Twice he thought his Marshals would at least encircle Bagration's force, but on each occasion that wily veteran of retreats had slipped away, once through the incompetence of Napoleon's own brother (Jerome) and once because his outriders had given him sufficient warning of Davout's approach for him to change his line of march. But Barclay's army would be a better prize; and preliminary skirmishes over the week-end of 25–26 July around Vitebsk convinced Napoleon that the Russians were prepared for a great battle. At ten o'clock on Monday night he left Murat with the melodramatic injunction, 'Till tomorrow at five – the sun of Austerlitz.'

Yet by five on the Tuesday morning there was no sign of Barclay's army except the glowing embers of its camp-fires. Barclay had indeed intended to offer battle at Vitebsk, but only if his troops were reinforced by the arrival of Bagration and the Second Army. Without Bagration, Barclay preferred to pull his men quietly away towards the massive walls of Smolensk, tempting Napoleon farther and farther into Russia. Momentarily, Napoleon hesitated: perhaps he might stay at Vitebsk and advance on Moscow or St Petersburg in the following spring, for the pace of the march was proving too

Napoleon directing
the battle of
Smolensk, 1812.

great for some of the non-French regiments and he was alarmed by
the figures of stragglers and deserters. But it was impossible to halt
the great machine moving so cumbersomely over the eastern plains.
Still he hoped for that one decisive battle.

It nearly came at the approaches to Smolensk on 15 August. The
First and Second Russian Armies had at last met and, although they
were still outnumbered by the French, there was a reasonable chance
that a surprise counter-attack against a tired invading force might
achieve more than a local victory. Barclay seriously considered such
an operation, but the lessons of Friedland were against him, and he
was painfully aware of Bagration's contempt for his authority. He
preferred instead to send Bagration eastwards with 60,000 men,
while he fought a delaying action at Smolensk, hoping that its
formidable ramparts would considerably weaken Napoleon's forces.
The Russians resisted for a day and a half of grim fighting in which
the French gunners bombarded the city for thirteen hours, setting
fire to the wooden houses of the inner town. General Philippe de
Segur later described how, as darkness fell on 17 August, the wind
seemed to make each individual burning building leap towards its
neighbour 'forming one vast blaze which, whirling about as it rose,
covered Smolensk, and entirely consumed it, with a dismal roaring'.
And Sir Robert Wilson, who had joined Barclay's army as a British
observer a few days earlier, commented in his diary on the wrath
and indignation felt among the Russians that such a city should be

destroyed unnecessarily: the rank and file of the First Army were eager by now to fight it out with the invader. They found the long withdrawal demoralising, especially as Barclay lost his way in the woods east of the burning city on the first night of the new retreat and was fortunate to escape encirclement on the banks of the Dnieper.

Napoleon had declared in a private conversation with Metternich at Dresden in the spring that he had no intention that year of advancing any further into Russia than Smolensk; and, as he established himself in the ruins of the citadel, he again considered suspending operations until 1813. But smouldering Smolensk offered his weary troops no real sanctuary. The weather was now extremely warm and the ground hard: he was tempted to press forward for a great cavalry battle before the coming of the autumn rains. Moreover, reports suggested that there was friction and intrigue within the Russian command: it seemed folly to Napoleon not to strike at such a moment.

On the very night that Smolensk was burning, Tsar Alexander – three hundred and fifty miles away in St Petersburg – reluctantly took a momentous decision. Yielding to pressure from some of his most trusted advisers, he dismissed Barclay from the high command

French soldiers watch the burning of Smolensk from the walls of the city on the evening of 18 August 1812.

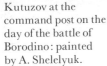

Kutuzov at the
command post on the
day of the battle of
Borodino: painted
by A. Shelelyuk.

and appointed Kutuzov as Generalissimo, with Bennigsen as his
chief of staff. Although the memory of Austerlitz still prevented
Alexander from showing trust in the old Marshal, the appointment
was extremely popular. Barclay's name was foreign, and he preferred
to talk in German rather than in any other language. But Kutuzov
was Russian to the core; and there was no alien affectation about
'the old fox of the north'. As Clausewitz wrote in later years: 'A true
Russian, a lesser Suvorov, exorcised the evil genius of the foreigners;
and no one doubted that soon the battle would take place which
would bring the French offensive to a halt.'

Kutuzov arrived at headquarters on 19 August. He found that
Barclay had taken up positions astride the main road to Moscow,
some thirty miles east of Vyazma and nearly a hundred miles west of
the old capital itself. It was tempting to await the arrival there of
Napoleon's forces, but Kutuzov was not going to be hustled into the
engagement which everyone by now anticipated. He confirmed
Barclay as commander of the First Army, Bagration as commander of
the Second; and ordered both of them to fall back to a section of the
plain which he had noticed between Gzhatsk and Mozhaisk, open
country broken by ravines and a shoulder of high ground on the
edge of a birch forest. Kutuzov did not even know the name of the

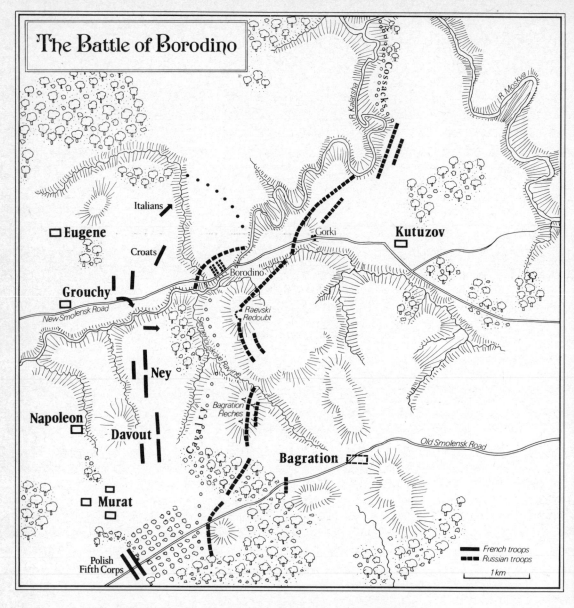

The Battle of Borodino

Italians

Croats

Eugene

Grouchy

New Smolensk Road

Ney

Napoleon

Davout

Murat

Polish
Fifth Corps

Borodino

Gorki

Kutuzov

Raevski
Redoubt

Semenovskoye Ravine

Cavalry

Bagration
Fleches

Bagration

Old Smolensk Road

R. Kalatsha

R. Moskva

Cossacks

French troops
Russian troops

1 km

place, but he had seen that it was close to the monastery of Kolot-skoye, and when he reached the position with the army on 1 September, he discovered that the village was called Borodino. Confidently he wrote to the Tsar, informing him that this was where he intended to give battle to the enemy. It was slightly over seventy miles west of Moscow.

At St Helena, looking in retrospect on his campaigns, Napoleon referred to Borodino as 'the most terrible of all my battles'. It was also, in many respects, the strangest of his victories, for it was an engagement in which there was little manoeuvre, but far more concentrated frontal assaults and much greater use of artillery on

The battle of Borodino as it appeared in the Soviet film *War and Peace*.

both sides than in any previous battle. Neither Napoleon nor Kutuzov displayed tactical skill at Borodino: Napoleon, who was suffering at the time from acute dysuria, showed excessive caution, rejecting Davout's proposal for turning the Russian left flank and refusing Murat and Ney the reinforcements which alone could have made Borodino as decisive as Austerlitz had been; and Kutuzov, who had expected the main enemy thrust to fall on his right flank rather than on his left, tended to be remote from the fighting, waiting on the 'New Road' through the villages of Borodino and Gorki for an assault which did not come. Some of the heavy casualties were caused by a lack of inspired leadership, but even more by the sheer weight of fire-power in the rival armies. Numerically the Grand Army (with about 130,000 men) outnumbered Kutuzov's force (110,000 trained troops, supplemented by 10,000 from the Moscow militia), but Napoleon had 587 field guns against Kutuzov's 640, many of them sited in prepared redoubts. Under these conditions, a fluid battle similar to Austerlitz or Friedland was virtually impossible, unless

Napoleon watching the battle of Borodino from the heights of Shevardino: Painting by Vereschagin.

the rival cavalry could break through on one or other of the flanks.

Just as Austerlitz was preceded by Bagration's action at Schön-graben, so Borodino was anticipated by a grim contest for the out-lying Russian redoubt at Shevardino on 5 September. After three hours fighting the hill at last seemed in French hands, but for another four hours the Russian cavalry disputed possession, although the infantry could make no progress. Only as dusk fell were the Russian survivors ordered to retire on the main defences by their commander, Bagration (to whom, once again, had fallen the task of making first contact with the enemy). The Shevardino action, in which the twelve Russian cannon had caused frightful havoc among Murat's horsemen, made Napoleon 'fall into a deep meditation' (said Segur) and may well have contributed to his hesitancy during the main battle two days later.

Borodino began at six in the morning of 7 September when a hundred guns on the French right opened fire on Bagration's Second Army. The cannonade was taken up by Eugene Beauharnais's Italian gunners two miles to the north, and then by the French centre. As the Russians answered back, the whole battlefield was soon covered by a reeking cloud of smoke which merged with the morning mist, confusing attackers and defenders alike. For eight hours over a thousand guns thundered along the ravines, making such a constant roar that survivors could not remember the crackle

The half-demolished village of Semyenouskoye; part of a Soviet model of the battle of Borodino.

160

of musketry or the call of bugles, responding only to signal rockets and the beckoning arms of their officers. No previous battle had produced such a terrifying volume of sound.

The first cavalry in action should have been the Polish Fifth Corps of the Grand Army, on the extreme right. But the Poles became entangled in brushwood and the earliest hand-to-hand encounters were reported half a mile nearer the centre of the line, where Davout personally led an assault on the fortified hill known as the 'Bagration Flèches'. Davout was seriously injured and the French made little impression on the Flèches, nor was Ney's attack on the position any more successful two hours later, the Russian twelve-pounders firing grapeshot down on lightly armed Württemberg troops, caught without shelter on the slopes of the mound. After a third unsuccessful attempt to seize the Flèches, Napoleon, watching the action from Shevardino, gave orders for four hundred guns to be concentrated on this one knoll. Bagration urged his weary men forward into a counter-attack, but as the two armies were locked in a hideous duel with bayonets, a splinter of grapeshot from one of the French batteries caught Bagration in the leg as he sat astride his horse. With magnificent courage he remained in the saddle, until weakness from loss of blood caused him to slip slowly to the ground. Still conscious, he was hurried off the battlefield (and, indeed, survived for another seventeen days) but knowledge that he had been gravely wounded

Overleaf left The holy city of Moscow, home of innumerable churches, cathedrals and monasteries.
Overleaf right above Rowlandson's cartoon of Napoleon watching the fire of Moscow.
Overleaf right, below The holy city seen from a distance, the fire gathering momentum.

161

spread dismay among the hard-pressed Russian soldiery, and they were forced back over the hill to the partial shelter of the Semenou-skoye Ravine. Without Bagration, there was no one left to rally them: 'The soul itself was gone from the whole of our left wing,' declared one of the Russian officers, looking back on the morning's fighting in later years.

Twelve hundred yards to the north, the centre of the line was dominated by a second hill on which the Russians had sited another battery of twelve guns, protected by a palisade and deep trenches. This position is sometimes known as 'the Great Redoubt' but more often as 'Raevski's Redoubt', from the name of the general commanding that crucial sector of the line. It proved an even more formidable obstacle than the Bagration Flèches. An initial assault by the French soon after ten in the morning made little impression on the outer defences. An hour later the French tried again and actually entered the redoubt itself before being thrown back by a furious Russian counter-charge, which cost the French fifteen hundred casualties. Soon after noon, pressure on the redoubt was relieved by a flank attack launched by the Russian cavalry reserve and the Cossacks on the Grand Army's left, at a point manned by Italian and Croatian defenders. The sight of seven thousand horsemen bearing down on them caused temporary panic, and the Italians and Croats fell back to the second line of French positions, held by General Grouchy, an extremely valiant and resourceful corps commander, with the experience of twenty years (and almost as many wounds) behind him. The Russians hesitated, halted, and never recovered the impetus of their assault: it was, for them, the supreme lost opportunity of the day.

Early in the afternoon the French made one last effort against the Raevski Redoubt, sending a cavalry corps over the open country on the southern slope of the hill and then swinging sharply to the left so

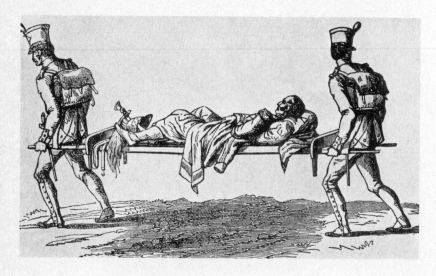

Stretcher bearers in the Napoleonic wars.

In Tolstoy's novel, Prince Andrew was taken to the camp infirmary after being wounded at Borodino.

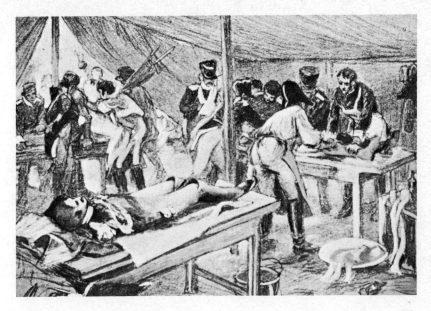

as to take the position in the rear before ordering the infantry to scale the mantraps and parapets which had wrought such terrible havoc during the morning. By three o'clock the Redoubt was at last in French hands; and the Russians fell back to their second line of defence, a thousand yards behind the positions they had held when the bombardment began nine hours earlier. Had Napoleon been prepared to risk his Old Guard, he might have finished off the Russians as drastically as at Friedland; but he was alarmed at the extent of his casualties and bitterly conscious of his isolation, especially if the Russians brought up further reserves from the south. 'I will not have my Guard destroyed eight hundred leagues from Paris,' he told Murat. The French still had to beat off desperate Russian counter-attacks, but, by the end of the afternoon, rain and mist settled on the battlefield. The weary armies suspended operations, and took stock of their losses.

Over 30,000 soldiers of the Grand Army were killed that day, including ten generals and another ten colonels. Kutuzov may have lost as many as 43,000 men, more than a third of his army. Both sides claimed a victory: Napoleon, because he was left master of the field; Kutuzov, because he still held the main route to Moscow at the end of the day. Moreover, he maintained that the losses imposed on the Grand Army were relatively of greater significance since it was so far from its bases. Briefly Kutuzov genuinely considered renewing the assault on the French next morning. Napoleon's troops, however, now held the better positions and his own guns, though heavier than the French, were less mobile. On reflection, he resolved to resume the retreat. In the small hours of 8 September, with a heavy mist over Borodino and the surrounding countryside, the Russian army began to fall back on Moscow.

7 The Triumph of Kutuzov

Count Rostopchin, the Civic Controller of Moscow at the time of the great fire of 1812.

Géricault's vision of the retreat of Napoleon's Grande Armée.

THE ENORMOUS EXTENT of the Russian lands and the distances separating one town from another meant that all reports from the battlefront travelled slowly. It is not surprising that couriers from Napoleon's headquarters took a fortnight to let Paris know of Borodino: the delay within Russia itself is more remarkable. A despatch sent by Kutuzov on the evening of Monday, 7 September, did not reach St Petersburg until the following Friday. It informed the Tsar there had been a major encounter between the two armies and that 'we remained masters of the field of battle'. Alexander at once assumed his troops had won a victory, and he publicly announced the news at a service in the monastic church of Alexander Nevsky. For over twenty-four hours there was great rejoicing, with fireworks and illuminations and constant pealing of church bells. People amused themselves by speculating where Napoleon would be imprisoned when he was brought captive to the capital. Next day Kutuzov's wife received a brief letter from her husband: 'My dear, I am in good health, thank God, and I have not been beaten; and I won the battle with Bonaparte.' But the note was sent from a position *east* of Mozhaisk, the last major town between Napoleon and Moscow. By Saturday evening doubt was spreading disappointment and dismay through St Petersburg: if Mozhaisk had been abandoned to the French, it was hard to see how Borodino could be acclaimed a victory for Russian arms. Alexander's personal prestige suffered a bad blow; and for the following three months he was reluctant to show himself in public.

In Moscow, too, there was consternation. A solemn *Te Deum* was offered for the success of Kutuzov's troops on Wednesday, 9 September. But that night the people of the city could see the glow of camp fires on the horizon and heard that Kutuzov himself was no more than twenty-five miles away. Civil control of Moscow was the responsibility of the Governor-General, Count Theodore Rostopchin (1763–1826). Once, as Tsar Paul's foreign minister, Rostopchin championed a French alliance but now his actions were fired by an

'Council of War at Fili'; an illustration for *War and Peace* by V. Serov; Marshal Kutuzov stands on the right.

almost hysterical patriotism. The Muscovites had become accustomed to broadsheets and caricatures alerting them to the need for service to the Tsar. They had watched him hustling the French community out of the city or parading wretches whom he claimed to be 'French prisoners' through the streets. When, on 11 September, Rostopchin called on the people of Moscow to arm themselves, gather on the road to Mozhaisk and follow him against the French, thousands of peasants and townsmen took him at his word, 'Immortal Glory to those who die in battle,' his proclamation declared, 'damnation till Doomsday for those who fail to come.'

Unfortunately, among the men who did not keep their appointment with destiny that day on the Mozhaisk Road was Rostopchin himself: he was always inclined to live his life at a lower pace than his rhetoric. After waiting for him until dusk, the Muscovites returned to their families, disinclined henceforth to respect the Governor or his authority. Most of them chose to evacuate the city, rather than risk the perils of a French occupation, and throughout the weekend of 12–13 September hundreds of carts, wagons, carriages, tumbrils and litters poured down the roads to Yaroslavl, Vladimir and Ryazan. Accompanying them were many of the wounded from Borodino, including the dying Prince Bagration.

Kutuzov arrived at the approaches to Moscow early on Sunday, 13 September, and spent most of the day in the village of Fili, five miles east of the Kremlin. He discussed the situation with Rostopchin in the morning, still uncertain whether or not to give battle outside the old walls. Rostopchin himself wrote two contradictory accounts of what they said to each other, but it would appear that while the Governor of Moscow wanted a delaying action on the last hills before the city, Kutuzov was disinclined to sacrifice lives for a token gesture of resistance. On that Sunday afternoon Kutuzov summoned all his leading staff officers to a conference in a peasant's cottage at Fili. Most of them appear to have wished to stand and fight for the defence of Moscow. Barclay (who was still technically Minister of War as well as a subordinate commander) agreed with Kutuzov over the need to conserve troops and material: he was prepared, if necessary, to go on retreating to the Volga. At last the decision was left to Kutuzov: 'You are afraid of falling back through Moscow,' he said to the young fire-eaters among the generals, 'but I consider it a providential way to save the army. Napoleon is a torrent which we are as yet unable to stem. Moscow will be the sponge that will suck him dry.' He ordered the army to retreat through the city, and to take the southern route for Kaluga. In the small hours of the morning Kutuzov himself was led through six miles of back streets by one of his equerries, for though he had confidence in what he was doing, he did not wish to see his troops passing through the centre of 'Holy Moscow'; and equally he had no desire for others to see him there. People later remembered that Monday as a 'beautiful summer's day'; but for Russia it was one of the blackest in her history.

The Grand Army reached the hills west of Moscow at noon on Monday, 14 September: officers and men were fascinated by the rich colour of the roofs and cupolas beneath them. Segur describes how Napoleon's Marshals, 'drunk with the enthusiasm of glory', crowded round their Emperor to offer him congratulations. In eighty-two days his troops had advanced five hundred miles from the river Niemen; but he was not entirely at ease. 'Here at last is the famous city,' he exclaimed, according to Segur. But he added, 'It is high time.'

Overleaf A contemporary engraving of Napoleon and his troops in the Kremlin, watching, with considerable alarm, the spread of the fire.

Napoleon spent his first night in Moscow at the Borogomilov Gate and did not ride to the Kremlin until the Tuesday morning. Although he was much impressed by the wealth of the Tsar's treasures, he was disappointed to find the city almost deserted. No person in authority had surrendered Moscow, for Rostopchin and all the

169

great families had joined the eastward migration. Already, too, on that first night fires were reported, though they appeared to have died down by the following morning. They were to grow in intensity as darkness fell again. Soon after midnight new fires broke out in widely separated districts of the city, and the first incendiarists were caught by French guards. The wind veered from north to west and at four o'clock on Wednesday morning, his aide-de-camp woke Napoleon, for the Kremlin itself seemed in danger. By now the occupying army had discovered that Rostopchin had destroyed or removed the few fire-pumps and hoses which the city possessed; and Napoleon's staff were convinced that Moscow had been assigned to the flames by order of its former Governor. 'A demon inspires these people,' Napoleon declared. 'They are Scythians! This is a war of extermination. What a people! What a people!' At four in the afternoon, Napoleon himself was forced to escape from the Kremlin and take refuge in the Petrovsky Palace, a couple of miles outside the city, on the road to St Petersburg.

The Great Fire of Moscow burned for four days and destroyed three-quarters of the city. There is still, even today, doubt over how it started. The Russians, at the time, believed the French had deliberately ravaged Holy Moscow, and this conviction intensified

Napoleon rides through Moscow inspecting the havoc caused by the fire: Painting by Delilla.

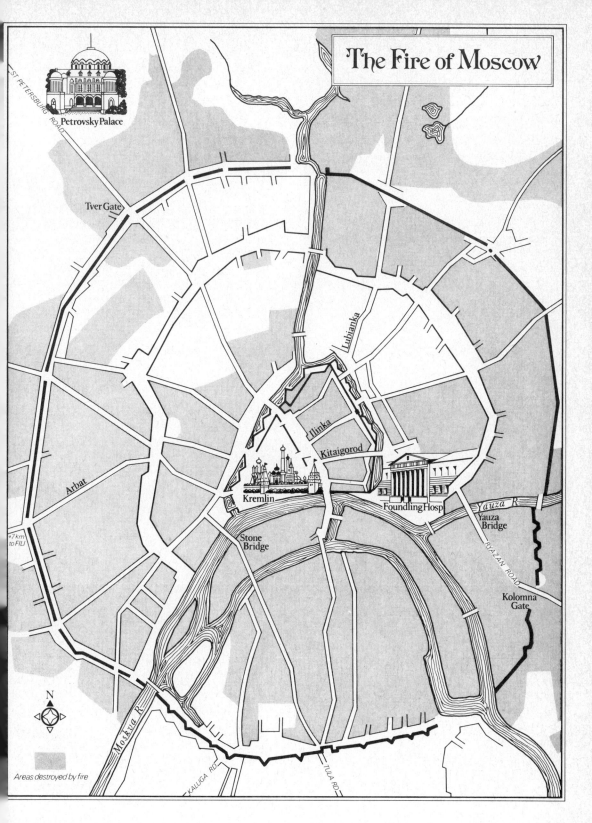

The Fire of Moscow

ST PETERSBURG ROAD

Petrovsky Palace

Tver Gate

Lubianka

Ilinka

Kitaigorod

Kremlin

Foundling Hosp

Yauza R.

Yauza Bridge

RYAZAN ROAD

Arbat

7 km to FILI

Stone Bridge

Kolomna Gate

N

Moskva R.

KALUGA RD.

TULA RD.

Areas destroyed by fire

the patriotic fervour of the nation throughout the coming winter. Yet tually prepared to leave the city, Napoleon did indeed order Marshal Mortier to blow up the Kremlin (a task only partially executed); but it is inconceivable that the French should, in September, have wished to burn their new base and the shelter on which they relied for the wintry months ahead. There is no doubt, on the other hand, that Count Rostopchin fired his own estate outside Moscow rather than have it fall into French hands, that he supervised the sabotage or removal of the fire-fighting materials from Moscow during the evacuation, and that he made several cryptic remarks to his family that indicated he would not be surprised to find the city erupting into flame. Fuses and incendiary devices were found in houses entered by the French before the fire reached them, and many of the sinister figures captured by Napoleon's patrols during the night hours were undoubtedly arsonists. Some fires were, however, certainly started accidentally after drunken carousing by the troops: this had already happened in the small town of Dorogobuzh when the French passed through during the last week in August. The risk of a small fire turning into a major conflagration was considerable in any Russian city at this time of year, as Rostopchin knew from long experience. His responsibility would seem to have been greater than that of anyone else.

Previous page left
Cruikshank's cartoon entitled 'Snuffing out Boney' conveys the image of primitive strength which the victorious Russian troops inspired in their enthusiastic British audience.
Previous page right, above
Russia's victory over Napoleon heralded a new era of Russian life, marked in particular by full participation in European political affairs and a new

Left The execution of Muscovites convicted of arson by Napoleon's troops: Painting by Vereshchagin.

Right Denis Davidov, the guerilla hero of the relentless partisan sorties on Napoleon's retreating troops.

awareness of Western ideas. But its immediate result was a sense of joyful release among the Russian people. Everywhere there were scenes of elegant recreation and reunion of officers with their families such as this engraving of the gardens of the Peterhof Palace. *Previous page right, below* Contemporary cartoon by Terebenev illustrating Russian harassment of the fleeing Napoleon.

Even before the fire, Napoleon had hoped the occupation of Moscow would end the campaign. He was convinced the city was such a prize that Alexander would sue for peace as soon as it was in French hands; and now it was so desolate, he was himself anxious for an early settlement so that he could lead his army back to its bases before the coming winter. For the moment, military operations were virtually suspended. Murat's cavalry patrols roamed over the countryside immediately east of Moscow without making contact with Kutuzov; and it was not until Napoleon had been in the city for nearly a fortnight that he realised the principal Russian army was south-west of Moscow, towards Kaluga, and in a position to threaten his communications with Smolensk and Vilna. But Napoleon was so confident of peace that he was not, at first, disturbed by Kutuzov's manoeuvre. Two Russians who had remained in the city were despatched to St Petersburg with separate messages for the Tsar: Napoleon did not offer peace; he merely hoped that Alexander would respond to the brotherly hand which, once again, he held out to him, as one sovereign to another. But the Tsar had sworn he would never negotiate with Napoleon so long as a single invading soldier remained at large on Russian soil; and this resolution Alexander was determined to keep. No reply was made to Napoleon's blandishments.

Strategically the French were ill-placed in Moscow, as Napoleon knew well enough. Kutuzov was to the south-west of them, with his headquarters near Tarutino, north-east of Vitebsk ominously poised above Napoleon's thin line of communication. Tormassov and the Third Army were still engaged in desultory operations against the Austrians, south of the Pripet Marshes; and in the fourth week of September, Tormassov received between thirty and forty thousand reinforcements from 'the Army of Moldavia', which had previously been fully occupied on the Turkish Front. While the Russians were thus steadily augmenting their forces, the French found their resources severely strained. Quite apart from casualties and desertions, the effectiveness of the Grand Army as a fighting unit was reduced by the need to garrison towns and strategic points along its five-hundred-mile route to Germany and the heart of the French Empire. Hence, in Moscow itself, Napoleon commanded rather less than 100,000 men; and he was easily outnumbered by the Russians on his flanks. At the end of September a partisan detachment under Colonel Denis Davidov (the prototype of guerrilla leader on whom Tolstoy modelled his 'Denisov') intercepted a force of eighty French dragoons more than a hundred miles west of Moscow and all were killed or captured. It was an ominous development; and Napoleon knew he could not ignore the pressure building up on either side of

Vereshchagin's painting of Napoleon in the midst of his dilemma after the fire of Moscow. His decision to retreat by the same route as he had come could not have been more ill-advised.

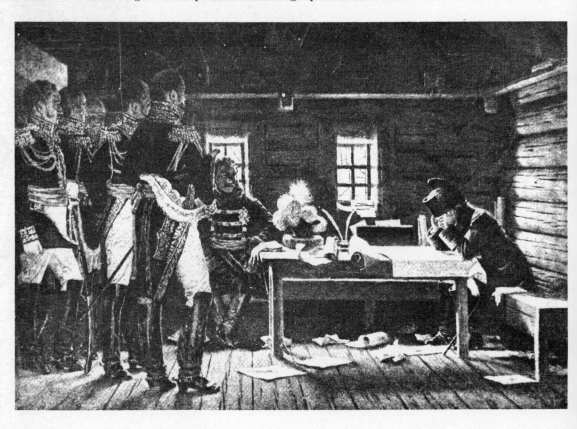

his tenuous link with the West. Early in October he sent Lauriston, a former ambassador in St Petersburg, to Kutuzov's headquarters with a letter for the Tsar. But the only effect of these repeated attempts to start negotiations was to encourage both Alexander and Kutuzov: every day that Napoleon stayed in Moscow was weakening his position; and bringing winter nearer. The sponge, as Kutuzov had prophesied at Fili, was gradually sucking the torrent dry; but as yet it had not entirely absorbed the French flood, and from time to time sharp skirmishes against the outposts of the Grand Army kept its commanders alive to the Russian presence.

On 18 October there was a severe clash at Winkovo nar Tarutino, in which a Russian cavalry raid led to some 2,500 French casualties. News of the action finally made up Napoleon's mind to leave Moscow, although he had already made the first moves to fall back on Smolensk a few days earlier. He decided that, rather than lead his men through ravaged fields and villages along the old line of advance, he would follow a more southerly route, where there was a better prospect of finding food and fodder. If the road to the south-west took the French directly towards the main Russian army, so much the better. Napoleon preferred to destroy the enemy concentration before falling back. Moreover, it might be possible to save face by going as far south as Tula, destroying the Russian arms factories and then wintering in Smolensk and Minsk. If Tula were left in ashes, it would be difficult for Alexander to continue the campaign in 1813. On Monday, 19 October, Napoleon crossed the Moskva River and set out south-westwards. He had lingered exactly five weeks in Moscow.

In one of the most moving passages of *War and Peace* Tolstoy describes how Kutuzov is woken from half-sleep at his headquarters near Tarutino and informed that, four days previously, the invaders had left Holy Moscow: the old Marshal sends for the young officer who brought the news that the French army was already at Forminskoie and, after questioning him eagerly, turns to the ikons on the wall and offers up a simple prayer of thanks to the Lord for having saved Russia. Although there is no record of Kutuzov's reaction to the great news, the scene Tolstoy described is based upon an historical episode. A Cossack horseman brought the old Marshal the momentous information that Napoleon was no longer in Moscow: General Docturov's patrols had encountered the main body of the French moving southwards towards Kaluga; and they captured an officer who confirmed that Moscow was evacuated. It is probable that Kutuzov did, indeed, thank God for the salvation of the old capital; but the presence of so large a force within twenty miles of his headquarters cannot have been entirely welcome to him, for his infantry was composed mainly of raw recruits who were, as yet, inadequately trained. He preferred once again to avoid a pitched battle, forcing

Napoleon to retreat while using the Russian superiority in horsemen to raid his columns.

A fierce engagement was, however, fought between the French and Russian vanguards, before the two principal commanders arrived. The town of Maloyaroslavets was built on a hill above the river Lutza, a small stream that cut its way through a series of ravines, crossed by a single bridge. Throughout Saturday, 24 October, Eugene Beauharnais's Corps (most of them Italian) disputed possession of the bridge and the town with a force of some 15,000 Russians, under General Docturov. Seven times between daybreak and dusk the town changed hands, the Russians losing one man in every three but receiving reinforcements later in the day. The wreck of Maloyaroslavets was left in Beauharnais's possession as darkness fell, and Napoleon's army bulletins subsequently spoke of the battle as a victory. But, in reality, it was the point where the French incursion into Russia was finally checked. Both the main armies declined to renew the conflict on the Sunday morning. The Russians could afford to fall back, using the geography of their country as a means of countering the enemy advance. For the French, withdrawal meant an acknowledgement that the Russian enterprise was too formidable even for the Grand Army.

Napoleon agreed to retreat only after two nights of hesitation and discussion with his marshals. On the Sunday morning he was nearly captured by a patrol of Russian Tartar cavalry (not, as was subsequently reported, by Cossack irregulars), but the Russians did not realise that they had encountered the French Emperor's own escort, and he was rescued by the Imperial Guard. It was a disturbing experience, even though he seems to have made light of it in conversation with Murat; and it may well have strengthened his decision to head directly for the West, where it was not so easy for raiding horsemen to appear unexpectedly, four or five miles behind his own advance-party. Almost to a man, his marshals advised Napoleon to fall back on Smolensk rather than pursue the elusive Kutuzov: the French cavalry horses were weary; the heavier gun-teams, hampered by the congestion on the narrow roads, could not keep up with the leading infantry regiments; and every day seemed to be getting darker and colder. At noon on Monday, 26 October, Napoleon finally turned his back on the Kaluga Road and set off from Maloyaroslavets for Mozhaisk and Smolensk.

When Maloyaroslavets was rebuilt by the Russians after the campaign, a small plaque commemorated the fighting of 24 October. It gave the date and added, quite simply, 'End of offensive, beginning of rout and ruin of the enemy.' Ultimately the claim was justified by events, but it was not until the end of the month that either Napoleon or Kutuzov fully realised the tide had turned. At first it seemed to both commanders that the French were undertaking an ordered strategic withdrawal. Napoleon, however, soon saw that the army

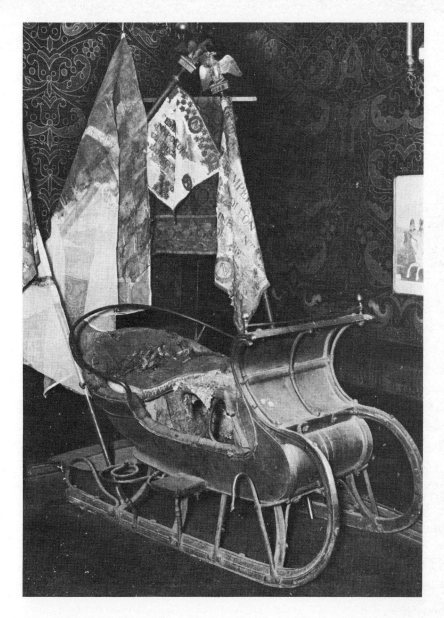

The sledge in which Napoleon travelled in his flight from Russia.

was making much slower progress than he had anticipated. It was encumbered by the mass of loot which was the only consolation to the soldiery for all the hardships of this frustrating campaign. Morale was low, and it is significant that within three days of leaving Malo-yaroslavets Napoleon was confiding to his closest companions that he now thought duty required him to pass the winter in the capital of his empire and not, as he had planned, at field headquarters in Poland.

The weather in these first days of retreat gave warning of winter's approach, but it was not so harsh as in the Austerlitz or Eylau campaigns. Much of the road was scarcely distinguishable from the adjoining fields after the heavy rains of autumn. By day, however, there was some pale sunshine. Only at night did the frost creep into the bones, ruthlessly exposing the inadequacy of western European uniforms. Food was becoming scarce and there was a terrible shortage of fodder for the horses, with little opportunity of relief so long as the route lay through villages devastated in July and August. Foraging parties rode out well to north and south of the line of retreat in search of supplies. But this was a dangerous practice: it meant further delays; and it exposed an isolated patrol to the rough justice of partisan resistance or the swifter vengeance of Cossack horsemen. Constantly, to the south of the line of retreat, there was a threat from the regular cavalry, under General Miloradovich (whom Davout himself described as 'the Russian Murat'). Twice Miloradovich's light horsemen struck at the French rearguard as they moved slowly towards Smolensk. Each time the weary columns suffered heavy losses, the survivors abandoning both loot and personal possessions in an effort to keep within the protective cover of the main body of men. The sight of decaying corpses exposed by the ruins and floods at Borodino was hardly calculated to boost morale. Even before the snow began to fall, the retreat had become a protracted nightmare for all forced to undertake it, whether soldiers, camp-followers or the wretched handful of prisoners.

Kutuzov wished to conserve his limited strength until he could make contact with the armies of Wittgenstein and Tormassov, west of Smolensk. He was, however, willing to shadow the French withdrawal, occasionally authorising Miloradovich and the cavalry to raid the long line of columns. Although he could not safeguard his troops against the rigours of the climate, he did at least ensure that they moved through areas not laid waste in the summer campaign. His chief military problem was the movement of guns and heavy wagons over the soft earth; but he was troubled by a political and social question – how far was it wise for him to encourage the formation of partisan guerrilla detachments? He was himself a landowner, worried like most of the nobility by the thought of a serf insurrection. One, at least, of the popular heroes thrown up by the patriotic resistance to Napoleon was a known trouble-maker, a private soldier who had been publicly flogged a few years previously: now, having escaped from French custody after the early skirmishes, he was raising the peasants in revolt aginst the invader. Should Kutuzov commend his enterprise? Or was there a danger that such a man would find it easy to rally the serfs against their masters once the foreign war was over? All too frequently partisan bands sprang up many miles ahead of Kutuzov's most advanced troops and yet expected him to send aid to them when they found themselves in a tight corner. Politically and strategically the partisans were an embarrassment, even though they were undoubted testimony to the

Napoleon's sometime 'Grande Armée' melted away during the dreadful march through the Russian winter, along an already plundered route, marked out by the dead of their earlier trek along the same road but in the opposite direction. (Still from the Soviet film *War and Peace*.)

growing sense of Russian national pride. To Kutuzov it was easy enough to determine what the Cossacks might do, for they had a hierarchical structure of their own; but guerrillas seemed to him a foreign importation, almost anarchic and hardly less damnable than the French themselves. The vengeance of the Russian peasantry was no part of his strategic plan: he preferred to be indebted to the Russian climate.

The first snow began to fall in the small hours of 4 November when Napoleon was still fifty miles east of Smolensk. His rearguard (Davout's First Corps) was, at the time, three days march away and under heavy attack from Miloradovich outside Vyazma. The full rigour of the winter did not set in until the night of 6–7 November and the next two days saw some of the worst blizzards of the campaign. Napoleon himself was forced to leave his carriage from time to time and, wrapped in a long Polish greatcoat, plodded through the snow as his riders and escort sought to lead their horses around the deep drifts at the ill-defined sides of the road. 'The snow came down in enormous flakes. We lost sight not only of the sky, but of the men in front of us,' wrote Sergeant Bourgogne, a veteran of the Imperial Guard. For eighteen hours Napoleon found shelter at a small post-house in a forest clearing somewhere east of Smolensk; and at last about noon on 9 November he was able to reach the city itself. Although so many buildings had been ruined in the bombardment and fire thirteen weeks previously, it still had enough roofs and rations to provide the desperately sick with shelter for a few days, but most of the army remained under canvas, and the late arrivals fared much worse than the Emperor's own escort. The Old Guard had even set up a fair in the centre of the ruined town, where they hawked some of the loot of Moscow in exchange for food and liquor, offering bales of Chinese silk or heavy ecclesiastical vestments for a bottle of brandy (of which there was an unexpectedly abundant supply in Smolensk).

The severe weather had taken even Kutuzov by surprise. He could not remember such intensive cold coming so early or so suddenly. The Russians called off all attempts at harassing the enemy while the blizzards were blowing, for although their horses were better shod than the French, it was rarely possible to see more than a few hundred yards ahead; the risk of tumbling into drifts was considerable. Moreover Kutuzov had no need to attack the straggling columns at this point. They were falling back into a giant trap, or so it appeared to the Tsar and his advisers around the maps at St Petersburg. Already Wittgenstein had re-taken Vitebsk, thus cutting Napoleon's route to Vilna and the supplies of Prussia and the Grand Duchy of Warsaw. To the south-west 'the Army of Moldavia' (commanded, a little unexpectedly, by an admiral, Pavel Chichagov) was advancing towards Minsk. Tormassov had handed over the Third Army to Chichagov and a formidable force was concentrating east of the Pripet marshes. It began to seem as if the Grand Army would be encircled on the formless ridges which mark the watershed between the Baltic and the Black Sea. All eyes rested on the long line of the river Berezina, which ran down the map from Wittgenstein's outposts in the north to join the Dnieper, east of the marshes. Here was a natural obstacle in the path of the retreating French.

Napoleon was fully aware of the gathering danger. He stayed only four days in Smolensk and then marched due west, convinced there was no imminent peril, for it did not seem to him likely that the Russians would maintain the pursuit. Musters taken before leaving Smolensk showed that he still had, under his command, some 50,000 effective troops and for the next stage of the retreat he divided them into four sections, each setting out one day after the other. Napoleon was with the Imperial Guard in the second section; and Marshal Ney brought up the rear. On the first day, despite icy roads and a series of low hills heavy with snow, Napoleon covered sixteen miles. Without either commander realising what was happening, his route was converging on Kutuzov's parallel advance; and at dusk on 15 November French and Russian headquarters were barely two miles from each other, nearer than they had been at any other moment in

The French banners are dipped before Kutuzov at Krasnoe. (Still from the Soviet film *War and Peace*.).

the campaign, even at Borodino. All that day and the next the French columns were attacked by Cossacks and raked by Miloradovich's cavalry and cannon near the town of Krasnoe; but, to the indignation of the émigré officers on his staff and of young hotheads like Davidov, Kutuzov refused to authorise a general attack. He dared not risk his troops against a commander of such genius under conditions which changed so rapidly from hour to hour. But by the time Ney and the rearguard arrived, Miloradovich blocked the line of retreat. The French were forced to make a detour northwards to the frozen Dnieper, crossing the thin ice on all fours, and eventually rejoining Napoleon on 20 November at the small town of Orsha. It had been a narrow escape from disaster.

At Orsha Napoleon heard that Minsk had been taken by Chichagov; and he knew at once that he must hurry for the Berezina. Three Russian armies – Kutuzov at his heels, Wittgenstein in the north, and Chichagov in the south-west – were now converging on the river. At Borisov there was a bridge carrying the road to Vilna. It was essential to reach Borisov before one or other of the Russian armies. Urgent messages were sent by fast-moving couriers to Marshal Oudinot, in command of the reserve depots, to march on Borisov; the Frenchmen were comparatively fit and well-disciplined and when they reached Borisov they had little difficulty in clearing the Russians from the town. In the fighting, however, the single bridge over the Berezina was fired and destroyed. It was by no means certain if there was anywhere to ford the river, which for much of its course ran between high banks or over swamps covered with thin ice. But local peasants informed Oudinot there was a possible crossing at Studenka, seven miles to the north; and a French reconnaissance party was sent out to discover if pontoon bridges could be erected at Studenka for the retreating columns, who were only a day and a half's march from the river.

The rank and file of the Grand Army was, by now, in a desperate state. Men suffered at one and the same time from frostbite and dysentery: they had hallucinations of food and drink, of the comfort of a warm hearth, of marching smartly past a saluting base in some parade of victory. With the rearguard there lingered pathetic stragglers, sometimes women and children, seeking protection from the Cossacks and partisans. There were instances of soldiers killing each other for possession of horse-flesh; and by now there were also grim tales of cannibalism. Between 18 November and the night of 23–24 November the snow held off, but when the main column of troops were thirty miles from the Berezina there was another sudden blizzard, which took a heavy toll of the weak and hungry horde. Yet the return of the frost improved the chances of getting the survivors

The crossing of the Berezina was the most ghastly incident in the struggle of the French army and its followers to retreat. This contemporary engraving by Solde captures some of the sufferings it inflicted upon exhausted men, many of whom drowned in the river.

across the river, for it thickened the ice and reduced the danger of a thaw causing the swamps to flood. Once the ice broke, there was no hope for anyone who fell into the swirling waters of the main stream.

Napoleon and most of the units of the Grand Army arrived on the left bank of the river in the early hours of 25 November. Deceived by an elaborate diversion, Chichagov thought the French intended to cross the Berezina some twenty miles south of Borisov and took up his positions accordingly. This ingenious feint did not give the French much more than a breathing space (for Wittgenstein's army was moving rapidly southwards down the river) but it enabled the untiring sappers to build two bridges at Studenka. Despite fire from the advance-guards of the Russian armies, most of Napoleon's men (including, by now, Oudinot's Corps) were able to cross the Berezina between the afternoon of 26 November and the night of 28–29 November: 50,000 troops safely reached the right bank of the river, but on the last day there were terrible scenes as the stragglers fought to cross the bridges before they were destroyed by the French rearguard. It is estimated that 15,000 people remained on the eastern bank of the river, pitifully huddled beside the dying embers of camp fires until the Cossack lances brought a cruel end to their misery.

There were eleven more days of retreat from the Berezina to the comparative safety of Vilna, and another three to the Niemen and the Prussian frontier. Only one man in ten out of the 50,000 who had crossed the Berezina reached the Niemen a fortnight later still identifiable as an efficient fighting man, although another 30,000 sick and wounded struggled back into Prussia by the end of the year. It was between the Berezina and the Niemen that the cold hit hardest, with the temperature falling to twenty-five degrees of frost. Napoleon personally left the army at Smorgonie on the evening of 5 December and set out, by carriage and sledge, for Paris, eleven hundred miles away. Rumours that the Emperor was dead in Russia had encouraged the growth of a conspiracy, and Napoleon felt it was essential for him to re-assert his control of the Empire. He arrived in his capital thirteen days later. By then a shattered rearguard had crossed into Prussia, harassed by Cossacks and partisans to the end. Marshal Ney, seeking to establish a defensive position along the frontier, reported to Napoleon at the beginning of 1813 that he had in all 40,000 men under his command. No one knows how many soldiers of the Grand Army failed to return from Russia, but the figure cannot be far short of half a million.

Kutuzov's army entered Vilna on 13 December. The old fox was happy. He had twice served as Governor of the Vilna region and it seemed to him a fitting place in which to celebrate his triumph. General Wilson, most of the Prussian émigrés and many of the Russian commanders themselves denied that Kutuzov had any cause for satisfaction. They complained that he had followed the

The image shows a printed cotton handkerchief with a decorative banner reading: "THE BATTLE of BEREZINA gained by the Brave RUSSIANS by Prince Kutusoff Smolensko. over the French No 28. 1812. with the flight of BUO commanded NAPARTE."

retreat too slowly, that he had hesitated at Krasnoe, and that he had allowed Napoleon to snatch safety from the trap at Borisov. The Tsar, too, was disappointed that there was no grand dramatic victory, with a captive Napoleon surrendering his sword. But Kutuzov had done what he intended. He had used the unique characteristics of Russia, its geography and its climate, as allies against the foreigner. Marshal Ney wrote in a letter to his wife: 'General Famine and General Winter, rather than Russian bullets, have conquered the Grand Army.' There was truth in his complaint, but it was Kutuzov who knew how to exploit these terrible companions-in-arms, just as it had been Kutuzov who had predicted that the occupation of Moscow would suck Napoleon dry. Strategy was for him a pragmatic art, never a science; and his victories were a triumph of common sense and experience.

The Russian survivors of the campaign spent the last fortnight of this memorable year at Vilna. The city, although undamaged

Cotton handkerchief printed in England in 1812 to commemorate the victory of the Russian allies at Berezina.

Overleaf Scene in a café in Vilna, December 1812. The usual gossip among barbers, writers and tea drinkers is dominated by the soldiers reports of Napoleon's humiliation, and the presence in the town of the triumphant Emperor Alexander and Marshal Kutuzov.

by the war, was a terrible sight. One of the Prussians in Alexander's service was horrified: 'The town looked like some Tartar hell, everywhere appalling dirt and smells,' he wrote. Sir Robert Wilson, who had accompanied Kutuzov into Vilna, commented in his diary on the sickness and diseases which were spreading from the French prisoners to the townspeople and to the Russian troops:

In fifteen days nine thousand prisoners have died, and in one eighteen hours seven hundred. . . . The physicians have ordered straw to be burnt before every house, but the pestilential atmosphere is not to be corrected by such palliatives. . . . I rode yesterday (29 December) round the town. . . . In all directions I saw mountains of human bodies, and carcases of beasts.

On days when the temperature climbed a few degrees and a thaw set in, the diseases seemed to spread even more rapidly. Wilson gloomily predicted that by the spring Vilna would be 'a complete charnel-house'.

Yet it was to this dismal scene that Tsar Alexander came to celebrate the liberation of his empire from the invader. He arrived from St Petersburg on 23 December, three days before his thirty-fifth birthday. Outwardly he greeted his commander-in-chief affably and commended his triumphs, investing Kutuzov with the Order of St George, First Class. Privately, however, it was clear the tension between the two men remained as strained as ever. Alexander did not hesitate to let foreigners like Wilson know that he thought Kutuzov 'has done nothing he ought to have done' and complained, 'all his successes have been forced upon him'. So long as the war continued nobody would again induce the Tsar to leave military headquarters. At sixty-seven Kutuzov seemed far older than his years, for the privations of the campaign severely taxed his strength, but the Tsar had no intention of sending him back to St Petersburg. It was far easier for Alexander to pay outward respect to the old warrior than risk a conflict with 'the Moscow nobility' by treating Kutuzov in the cavalier fashion his father had accorded to Suvorov. It did not seem as if the marshal would survive to plague him much longer.

At times, however, the old man's stubbornness severely tried Alexander's patience. The Russian disaster had broken 'the spell of Napoleon' for all the subject peoples, as the Tsar himself said. During the campaign the Prussians and Austrians, though technically allied to the French, had not played a prominent part in operations. Now at headquarters in Vilna it was already becoming clear that Prussian officers were preparing to force King Frederick William to change sides; and there were signs that Metternich, too, would soon urge the Emperor Francis to break with his son-in-law. On the final day of 1812 General Yorck, who commanded 12,000 Prussians along the Baltic seacoast, concluded an arrangement with the Russians by which his troops would withdraw from the war. The Tsar began to see himself as the predestined liberator of Europe, a man of God called to settle the future of the continent. Once again, as before Austerlitz, he looked into a mirror and thought he recognised there the features of an impartial arbiter, noble in sentiment and wiser than his years. It was, however, an image which eluded Kutuzov. There seemed to him no reason why Russia should entangle herself in the affairs of Europe: now that the sacred soil was cleared of foreign soldiery, she should turn her back on the German lands. For the old Marshal – and for all true sons of Suvorov – the Empire's future lay in the East.

There were many Russians, then and later, who shared this belief. Why call more men to the colours and create new armies? Why impose more taxes? Why march on Paris, while Moscow and a trail of ruined towns and charred villages await rebuilding? To a large extent, Tolstoy agreed with this point of view: when he wished to end the historical narrative of *War and Peace*, he set the final scene in Vilna, with Kutuzov ordering the captured standards to be laid at the Tsar's feet; and, by this device, the novelist was able to leave the last chapters free for philosophic reflections and an affirmation of the happiness in family life contrasted with the unreal heroics of war. But for a quarter of a million Russian soldiers the delights of peace were still a year and a half away at the time of the Vilna ceremonies; for Alexander's sense of mission inevitably prevailed over the more limited objectives of the Kutuzov circle. On 15 January 1813 the Tsar sent his army westwards across the Niemen; a resounding proclamation spoke of freeing 'from misery and oppression even those peoples who took up arms against Russia'.

Alexander's troops were indeed welcomed in Prussia as liberators. Frederick William duly concluded an alliance and in March the Prussians formally declared war on France. Kutuzov had been unimpressed by the quality of the recruits who were reaching him from Moscow and St Petersburg; he was painfully conscious that when he accompanied the Tsar into Prussia he had fewer men under his command than in 1805, before the Austerlitz disaster. But it seemed as if Kutuzov's fears were unjustified. The French had no opportunity of holding the Grand Duchy of Warsaw and could not organise defences in Saxony. By the first week in April the Russo-Prussian allies had crossed the Elbe, entered Dresden in the south and sent out a raiding party to seize Hamburg in the north. There was, as yet, virtually no opposition: France appeared stunned by the disasters of the retreat from Moscow.

'We can cross the Elbe all right, but we shall re-cross it before long with a bloody nose,' Kutuzov had predicted in mid-March; and, though he did not live to see it, he was right. Napoleon spent the first months of the year raising a new army. By 15 April, when he left Paris, he had a quarter of a million men mustered west of the Main, short of horses and artillery but outnumbering the Allied force in

Thuringia by two to one. On 2 May the Allies launched a surprise assault on Napoleon at Lützen, but were so slow to develop their attack that the French snatched a victory and recovered Dresden a week later. At the end of the month there was another battle at Bautzen, where both the French and the Russians suffered heavy losses; but it was the Russians who pulled back, and for a moment it began to seem as if they were once more going to lose their position in Germany.

Kutuzov had died on 28 April, at his headquarters at Bunzlau in Prussian Silesia. Temporarily Alexander chose Wittgenstein as commander-in-chief but the appointment caused resentment among the 'pure Russians' and, after the battle of Bautzen, he resigned in favour of Barclay de Tolly, whom the Tsar hurriedly summoned from St Petersburg in the middle of May. In practice, however, Alexander insisted on taking all major strategic decisions himself: this was fortunate for the Russians since Barclay's first inclination after Bautzen was to advise the Tsar to fall back on Poland and, if necessary, establish a new line along the Russian frontier. He was depressed by the apparent resilience of the Grand Army; but Alexander remained convinced that Napoleon's cause was lost and he refused to give way to Barclay's pessimism.

Napoleon's position looked better than it was. He never succeeded in replacing the horses lost during the winter catastrophe and he was now short of ammunition and painfully conscious that his peoples were weary of war. Metternich, well-informed of the true state of France, proposed an armistice, and found both sides willing for a respite and by no means ill-disposed towards Austrian mediation. For ten weeks there was no fighting, a neutral zone of twenty-five miles separating the opposing outposts. Ultimately the armistice benefited the Allies more than the French: reinforcements arrived from Russia; and, as the French refused to accept Metternich's proposals for a general settlement, Austria, too, entered the war against Napoleon. By the end of the first week in August the Allies had mustered an army of 800,000 men in Germany (Austrians, Prussians, Russians and Swedes). Napoleon had, on paper, a force of 700,000 but many of his troops were raw recruits and the loyalty of the Bavarian and Saxon conscripts, still nominally in his service, was highly suspect.

It took seven months for this final coalition to overcome the French. At times it seemed as if Napoleon might still snatch a decisive victory and force a compromise peace. Alexander insisted, in the fourth week of August, on ordering a frontal attack on the city of Dresden, an appalling failure which cost the Allies 30,000 men, and there were other shocks and setbacks as the armies moved relentlessly towards Paris. But ultimately the sheer weight of men and material threw even Napoleon's tactical genius into eclipse. It was numbers more than military skill that won Leipzig for the Allies in mid-

"Brother the Lord is with us."

THE EMPEROR OF RUSSIA, KING OF PRUSSIA, AND THE EMPEROR OF AUSTRIA.

Spontaneously returning thanks in the Field of Battle after the Great Victory at Leipsic in 1813.

The Allied Monarchs, Emperor of Russia, King of Prussia and Emperor of Austria give thanks in their various religious traditions, Russian Orthodox, Lutheran and Catholic, for their victory on the field of Leipzig, 1813.

October, after sixty hours of intermittent fighting. Plagued by typhus and demoralised by retreat, the French were left on their own to guard the west bank of the Rhine as the coldest winter that anyone could remember swept down on Europe.

There was little cohesion or unity in the Allied camp. The Austrians insisted in August that, if they were to enter the war, the overall command of the Allied troops should be entrusted to Field Marshal Prince Schwarzenberg, a request which the Russians and Prussians only accepted with considerable reluctance. Less than a year previously Schwarzenberg had commanded the Austrian expeditionary force which kept the Russian Third Army pinned down in the region of the Pripet marshes. It was intolerable for the Russian generals to

The Russians
in Paris

Right The entry of
Alexander's troops into
Paris: a contemporary
French view.
Below Bivouac of the
Russian troops in the
Champs Elysées, 1814.

Right A young Russian
officer takes his leave
of a Parisienne.

Adieux d'un Russe à une Parisienne

find themselves subordinated to Schwarzenberg, and among the ordinary soldiery the old hatred of foreigners speedily re-asserted itself. There was an almost seditious song which had a nostalgic chorus ('Sing, brothers, of other times when Suvorov carried our banners forward') and asked the pertinent question, 'Where, today, are those leaders worthy to be called Suvorov's sons?' It was not difficult to find an answer. Kutuzov and Bagration were dead: and Miloradovich and Raevski were now expected to trail behind a cautious and corpulent Austrian. The Russian peasant soldiers resented this apparent slight on their military leaders.

It made little difference. Although Schwarzenberg was nominally the supreme Allied commander, all political decisions of consequence – and most strategic ones as well – were taken by the Tsar. His reputation bounded as his troops moved farther and farther into Europe, so that he became to many people an almost legendary hero, a mysterious saviour from the East. To writers in London he seemed 'the Agamemnon of our age', 'the new sun warming our dismal World'; and across the Atlantic the good people of Boston, Massachusetts, sent greetings from a public meeting to 'our wise and glorious Friend'. Alexander was exalted by all the adulation bestowed on him: it confirmed his resolve to press forward into France as soon as possible. When the Allied commanders hesitated over whether or not to cross the Rhine, it was the Tsar who spurred them on. And, in the last resort, it was he who insisted on marching directly on the French capital.

He had, it was clear, little use for a negotiated peace. 'The sword alone can and must decide the course of events,' he declared; and he infuriated his allies by adding disdainfully: 'You cannot expect me to come four hundred leagues every time you need help.' Metternich thought he was determined to avenge the destruction of Russia's old capital, and did his best to frustrate such a plan: 'Tsar Alexander believes it his duty to Moscow to blow up the Tuileries. They will not be blown up,' the Austrian Foreign Minister wrote back to Vienna in January 1814. Yet, in reality, the Tsar's intentions were far more honourable. From time to time, he still seemed to breathe fire and fury; but he calmed his wrath by reading and re-reading the Ninetieth Psalm. He sought vengeance only from Napoleon personally, never by pillaging the city of Paris. To pass the unfinished Arc de Triomphe or to set foot on the Pont d'Austerlitz was balm sufficient for all old wounds to his pride.

The Russians entered Paris on 31 March 1814, their sovereign resplendent in the green uniform of his Guards – with stirrups, epaulettes and collar of gold, and a massive hat worn sideways and surmounted by a sheaf of cock feathers. Napoleon abdicated on 6 April, and, for over a week, the Tsar was virtually custodian of France, keeping his troops under admirable discipline and restraining the less accommodating instincts of his Prussian ally. He remained in Paris for two and a half months thrashing out the preliminaries of a treaty of peace. Then he crossed the Channel to England, for victory parades and gala celebrations and an honorary doctorate at the University of Oxford. He left Dover for the long journey back to St Petersburg on 27 June. There was no doubt that the Tsar was the principal beneficiary from the downfall of Napoleon's empire. Less than two years previously he had thought his throne and his life in danger: now he was hailed by his subjects as 'Alexander the Blessed One'. Fortune had never before changed so rapidly for a ruler of Russia.

8 Epilogue: Tolstoy's Russia

Leo Tolstoy in 1855, an officer in the Crimean Wars.

TSAR ALEXANDER REIGNED for another eleven years after his return to St Petersburg. In peace as in war he remained a contradictory character, half dreamy idealist and half realistic politician. Increasingly in his later years he spent his days in reflective solitude, wrestling with spiritual problems troubling his conscience: 'The flames of Moscow lit up my soul,' he explained on one occasion to a Lutheran pastor. For all his love of parades and military showmanship, he hated the suffering and social disruption of war, and he never entirely forgot the enlightened ideas he had absorbed in his youth. When his police chiefs told him that dangerous revolutionary doctrines were spreading through the Russian cities he was reluctant to authorise action against the radicals. For a time he held out to his subjects the hope of introducing some parliamentary system into his lands. But ultimately he lacked the will to change the structure of the Empire, and nothing came of his moments of liberal enthusiasm. The last five years of Alexander's reign were bleak with repression.

The young officers who came back from the wars had learnt much from their contacts with the West. They were proud of the part played by Russia in the overthrow of Napoleon, but their patriotism was affronted by the blind ineptitude of the Government in the aftermath of war. Michael Bestuzhev-Ryumin, one of the most eloquent of the junior officers, explained a few years later how disillusionment spread among the Russian people after their high hopes of emancipation and liberty in 1812–13:

The appeal of the Russian Monarch resounded on the banks of the Rhine and the Seine. The war was still on when the soldiers, upon their return home, for the first time disseminated grumbling among the masses. 'We shed blood,' they would say, 'and we are forced to sweat under feudal obligations. We freed the Fatherland from the tyrant, and now we ourselves are tyrannized over by the ruling classes.' The army, from generals to privates, upon its return did nothing but discuss how good it is in foreign lands. A comparison with our own country naturally brought up the question, 'Why should it not be so in our own lands?'

Another Guards officer, finding society in the capital tedious after the freer atmosphere of the West, was hardly less outspoken:

It became unbearable to watch the empty life in St Petersburg, listening to the grey beards who lauded everything that was old and poured scorn on every progressive thought. We had left them a hundred years behind.

Moscow might be rebuilt according to the old pattern: Russia herself could never be.

By 1820 secret societies had begun to spring up among dissident groups within the army itself. Their leaders were men of courage and liberal conviction. One of the most important cells was headed by Colonel Pavel Pestel, son of a governor-general of Siberia, and himself wounded at Borodino while still only in his twentieth year. At first the secret conspirators wished to rid the Tsar of what they considered to be his 'evil counsellors', and in particular General Arakcheev. Later they began to formulate more ambitious plans, calling for a constitution and for emancipation of the serfs. Some were genuine radicals, daring to dream of a Russian republic; others continued to believe that eventually 'Alexander the Blessed' would recover his old enthusiasm for enlightened ideas. Many were confused over what precisely they should do and what they should seek. A few even plotted Alexander's assassination.

The dramatic events of December 1825 crystallised their fears and their resolve. At the end of September the Tsar had left St Petersburg to winter in the Crimea and southern Russia. Suddenly, in November, he contracted a chill and subsequently a fever, which confined him to bed in the small temporary palace at Taganrog, on the Sea of Azov. At the end of the month his condition worsened and on 1 December it was announced that he was dead. Eight days elapsed before the news reached St Petersburg.

For the next three weeks there was great confusion in Russia. Most people assumed that the new Tsar would be Alexander's brother, Grand Duke Constantine, who had an unmerited reputation for liberal sympathies. Many took their oath of allegiance to Constantine, who was at the time in Poland and did not come near the capital. In 1822 he had told Alexander of his determination to renounce the succession: all he wished to do was to go on living in Warsaw, with the Polish countess he had married in 1820. Alexander accepted Constantine's decision and signed a secret manifesto declaring his younger brother, Nicholas, to be heir-apparent. But in 1825 Nicholas had doubts of his own abilities and was among the first to swear allegiance to Constantine. Hesitation and recrimination between the brothers continued for more than a fortnight. The administrative chaos was too good an opportunity for the conspirators to miss. In the last week of December they determined to precipitate matters. If the brothers could not decide who ruled in St Petersburg, the Guards Regiments would settle the question.

Above left Grand Duke Constantine, second son of Emperor Paul, who renounced the throne in favour of his younger brother Nicholas: English caricature of 1826.
Above right Tsar Nicholas I of Russia.

On 26 December 1825 several of the Guards battalions in the capital mutinied, declaring themselves in favour of 'Constantine and a Constitution'. General Miloradovich, the legendary cavalry hero of 1812, tried to talk to the insurgent leaders but was shot dead in the back. Nicholas at last asserted his authority and was proclaimed Tsar. He had known there was a conspiracy in St Petersburg and in the southern provinces: and he was ready. Loyal troops were sent to the square in front of the Winter Palace. Three rounds of cannon fire broke the rebel lines, eighty soldiers lying dead in the snow. The rest were pursued by cavalry across the Neva towards the grim fortress of St Peter and St Paul which seemed, to at least one observer, to await greedily their coming. Attempts to raise rebellion in the south and seize Kiev failed no less dismally. The 'Decembrist Conspiracy', as people called it, was a pathetically wretched epilogue to the military glory of Alexander's reign.

The conspiracy had a strange sequel. Five Decembrists were executed, among them Colonel Pestel. Nearly a hundred received prison sentences or short periods of exile in the penal colonies of Siberia. Another thirty-one, most of them veterans of the march across Europe, were sentenced to life imprisonment with hard labour in Siberia. Twenty-nine of these unfortunates were still alive when Alexander II succeeded Tsar Nicholas in 1855. A year later those who wished to do so were allowed to return to European Russia, provided they

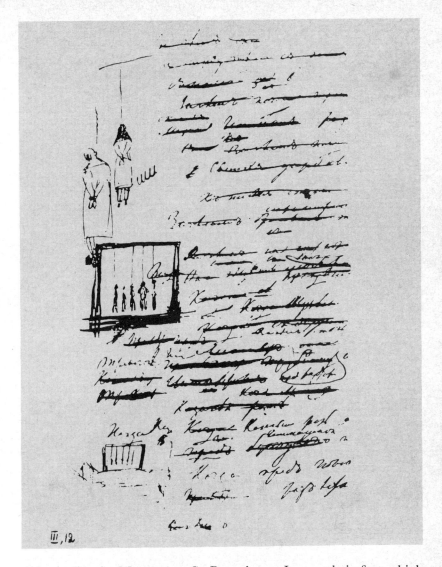

did not live in Moscow or St Petersburg. It was their fate which
stirred the imagination of a young writer, who had recently been
discharged from an artillery regiment after the siege of Sebastopol.
He began to plan a novel in which the hero was to have been one of
the Decembrists returning from Siberia, a man who in his youth had
fought through 'Russia's glorious period of 1812'. And it was thus
that a natural regression of historical sympathies prompted Tolstoy
to find, in the Odyssey of the Decembrists, a tale which became in
time the saga of *War and Peace*.

Leo Tolstoy was born in the early autumn of 1828 at Yasnaya
Polyana, a family estate of some 5,400 acres set in forested, hilly
country due south of the city of Tula and about 130 miles from
Moscow. His life spanned the most critical period in the history of

Tsardom, eight decades of frustrated hopes and disillusionment.
When he came into the world, less than three years had elapsed since
the Decembrist conspiracy. When he died, in November 1910, Russia
was only seven years short of the Bolshevik revolution. During his
lifetime the population of the Russian Empire leapt from 60 million
to 163 million. Russia became a stirring giant, but one shackled by
a dynasty and a Church which refused to look either at the present
or the future.

Tolstoy witnessed momentous changes in his eighty-two years. In
1861 the serfs were at last emancipated, although the reform imposed

The Russian serfs
were finally liberated
in 1861.

such a crippling burden of 'redemption debts' on the peasants that many suffered more privations after emancipation than under the old system. Other reforms of the 1860s also held promise, rarely fulfilled: the growth of secondary education, the introduction of elected assemblies in local government and of a modern code of criminal procedure and the substitution of conscription for the inequitable forced levy of army recruits. Gradually the essentially rural character of the vast Empire withered away, with new industries and improved communications opening up the interior. When Tolstoy was born serfs were still building Russia's first stone macadam trunk road, from Moscow to St Petersburg: they had begun it in 1816 and it was only finished, with the help of sapper battalions from the army, in 1833. And yet when he died it was possible to travel by railway from the Polish frontier to the Pacific coast.

There remained much in Russian life which offended Tolstoy's sense of human dignity, vitiating his genuine love of the country and its peoples. He deplored the activities of the 'Third Department' (the secret police) and all the clumsy attempts at suppressing written expression of original thought; and he was appalled to find Church dignitaries closing their minds to proposals of tolerance and compassion. Equally he disapproved of desperate terrorism and assassination, for social anarchism came nearer his temperament than violent revolution. Towards many of the changes in Russian life he remained an observer rather than a participant although he personally suffered from the cumbersome censorship and from obscurantist Orthodoxy. The Holy Synod of the Russian Church marked the opening of the twentieth century by formally excommunicating Tolstoy for his heterodoxy at a time when he was still searching for the true God in his heart. This action caused resentment throughout Russia and in many other lands as well; for thousands at home and abroad were hoping to find in Tolstoy's quest a faith to lift them from despair.

To one of the most significant developments of his lifetime, Tolstoy contributed as much as any other single person. From the early sixteenth century onwards Russia was primarily a recipient of Western culture, offering little in exchange except the beauty of a Church whose ritual and language few outside the Tsar's Empire could readily appreciate. But the last quarter of Tolstoy's life saw acceptance by the West of Russian culture, a recognition of the unique genius in Russia's writers and composers of music. By the end of the first decade in the present century Pushkin, Turgenev, Gogol, Herzen, Dostoevsky and Chekhov were all respected figures in a common European literary heritage, not simply distinguished foreign writers in translation. When Tolstoy first went as a young man to Moscow and St Petersburg he found intellectuals talking of German philosophy while society still slavishly imitated the cultural fashion of Paris, as in the days of Catherine II: and yet, in the last summer of his life, it was Paris that talked of St Petersburg and Moscow, of the 'essential Russianism' in Stravinsky's new *Firebird* and of what Stanislavsky was mounting for the theatre. If the cultural wheel had come full circle, it was *War and Peace* – an unfinishing symphony in historical imagination – which first set it in motion.

The Russia of *War and Peace* was outwardly hardly distinguishable from the Russia of Tolstoy's childhood and youth. It is true that by the beginning of the 1840s there was already a restless curiosity among a small minority of intellectuals, the new 'intelligentsia' enjoying the opportunities of travel in other lands and of study in foreign universities; but it was another twenty years before the pace of life in general began to quicken dramatically. Tolstoy spent a happy childhood, mostly in the countryside. Life for the peasantry at Yasnaya Polyana was better than at the turn of the century, but when Tolstoy inherited the estate in 1847 the workers on his lands and in the house were still bound in personal serfdom. There were, at that time, three hundred and fifty male serfs at Yasnaya Polyana, together with their families. Many of these retainers could remember the heroic days of 1812–13; and some were delightfully eccentric characters. Tolstoy happily tolerated Gasha, once his grandmother's maid, who extended a laudable love of animals to the least endearing creatures such as mice, cockroaches and spiders; and he was amused by a cook, who had once been a flautist in his grandfather's serf orchestra but was transferred to menial duties for losing his mouthpiece, a disaster for which he would console himself by bouts of heavy drinking and singing. Other serfs were less entertaining. When, as a landed proprietor of nineteen, Tolstoy tried to improve the welfare of the serf labourers in his fields, anticipating emancipation by more than a decade, he found every good intention thwarted by mistrust and suspicion: better the well-tried ways of old than these new-fangled notions of the young master. It was an experience which would find a place several times in Tolstoy's stories and novels.

Inevitably Yasnaya Polyana itself became an inspiration to a sensitive writer. Tolstoy used to keep a notebook with him in which he would jot down random facts, interesting scenes and unexpected marvels of nature. The very name of his estate suggests the fascination he felt for trees outlined against the open sky, for Yasnaya Polyana means 'a clear glade in a wood'. The long avenue of birch trees leading to a white mansion; the limes and the fruit blossom in the parkland; the reedy shallows and treacherous pools of the little river Veronka; the cavalcade of merchants, beggars, pilgrims, holy men and charlatans passing along the road beside the estate to Orel or Kiev – all these impressions from early years found their way into *War and Peace*, even if Yasnaya Polyana was in a quieter corner of Russia than the Bolkonsky lands east of Smolensk. Every summer for the rest of his life, Yasnaya was to call its master back.

Tolstoy as a student: Drawing by unknown artist.

Opposite An avenue in Yasnaya Polyana, Tolstoy's country home.

A group of contributors
to the magazine
Contemporary, founded by
Alexander Pushkin:
left to right Goncharov,
Turgenev, Druzhinin,
Ostrovsky. Standing at
the rear, Tolstoy
and Grigorovich.

But the young Tolstoy was too restless a spirit for the life of a
country gentleman. He soon tired of the administration of his estate.
For two years he studied, not over-diligently, at the University of
Kazan and then drifted to Moscow. There he gambled so recklessly
that one night he had to forfeit the original house at Yasnaya in
order to settle a debt. In 1851 he enlisted as an army cadet and saw
service in the Caucasus, where he came to know the Cossacks and to
hear the half-legendary tales they told of 1812–13. He was commissioned at last as a lieutenant of artillery, and he took part in the
defence of Sebastopol against the French, British and Piedmontese
throughout the winter of 1854–55 and the following summer. While
serving in the army he wrote three autobiographical studies which
showed such depth and insight into human nature that they created
a sensation; and it is said that when the new Tsar, Alexander II, read
them he gave orders for Tolstoy to be drafted out of the forward
gun emplacements, since it was essential to preserve his genius and
not risk his life under some random bombardment. Once the war was
over he retired from the army and enjoyed a social success at St
Petersburg. His knowledge of redouts, trench walls, batteries and
parallels was to help him describe Tushin's action at Schöngraben
and the day of Borodino; and it was reasonable for him to assume the

society small talk he heard in the capital had changed little between
one war against a Bonaparte and another, even though half a century
separates Austerlitz from Balaklava and Inkerman.

Already he was looking for a theme to fit the great work he felt
impelled to write, but as yet he was not ready for the task. Restlessly
he travelled in western Europe: in London he became a friend of
Alexander Herzen, twenty years earlier the revered prophet of
Hegelian philosophy in Russia, but now living in voluntary exile in
Paddington; and while in Brussels, he met the French social critic,
Proudhon, who had just completed a work entitled *La Guerre et la
Paix*, a Rousseauist essay in the paradoxes of Might and Right. By
the summer of 1862 Tolstoy was back in Russia, dividing his time
between Yasnaya and Moscow, and wrestling with deep inner conflicts of emotion. At last he made up his mind to seek a wife. In
September he proposed to Sofya Andreyevna Behrs and a week later
they were married in one of the churches of the Kremlin. The bride
was eighteen years old; Tolstoy had known her since she was eleven
and her mother since his own childhood. The couple settled at
Yasnaya Polyana for the winter; and in June 1863 a son was born,
and baptised Sergei.

Within a few weeks of the birth of his heir, Tolstoy settled down to

work on the novel he had already discussed in detail with his young wife. At times he travelled to Moscow and St Petersburg, to Smolensk and the towns and villages along the line of retreat. He spent two days in the summer of 1867 studying the terrain of Borodino, making his own sketch-maps, climbing to the rising-ground and looking out over the ravines from the knoll at Gorki, where he was to place Pierre in his novel. But for most of the time he lived at Yasnaya, writing in his library or in an outhouse. For more than six years 'Sonya' (as he called his wife) assisted him, copying out the manuscript many times over, handling his moods of elation and despair, sometimes working eight hours a day, and – if the evidence of Maxim Gorky and her own sister may be believed – providing him with the feminine response of his characters when his own imagination was sapped dry. Sonya lived out with her husband the life of the novel itself; and yet she could not, as he could, retire from the realities of day to day existence, if only because three more babies were born while the book was being written. It is hardly surprising that *War and Peace* is pervaded by the atmosphere of Yasnaya in the eighteen-sixties, or that the characters of Sonya and her sister, Tanya, brighten some of its warmest pages in thin disguise.

Sonya Tolstoy (*née* Sofya Behrs) whom Tolstoy married in 1862 when she was eighteen.

Tolstoy was fascinated by the recent past for at least ten years before his marriage and probably for longer. He appears to have read most of the French and Russian studies of the 1812–13 campaigns when he was at Kazan and Moscow, before his service in the army. It is not clear precisely when he decided to write an epic novel of his country's struggle in the early years of the century. On one occasion he said that the idea had come to him in 1856 and that he envisaged narrating 'a story with a definite tendency, the hero of which was to have been a Decembrist returning with his family to Russia' from exile in Siberia; and in a private letter to the great Herzen early in 1861 he says that he had written the first chapters at the end of the old year and read them to Turgenev, with whom he was at that time on terms of good friendship. But as the excitement over the return of exiled Decembrists died down, so Tolstoy looked farther and farther back for his opening scene until he found a situation full of anger, pride and over-confidence which seemed familiar to him. 'The first germ of interest in history arises out of contemporary events,' Tolstoy once declared; and it is easy to see how for him, and many of his generation, the Crimean War and the landing of the French and their allies on Russian soil inevitably stimulated reflection on the contest with the greater Napoleon early in the century. By the 1860s Austerlitz, Borodino and the fate of the Grand Army were as natural subjects for literate Russians as the First World War became to the reading public in Britain and America a hundred years later. It is small wonder that Tolstoy turned to 1805 and 1812 for the setting of the masterpiece he was determined to write.

He had, however, no desire to compose a conventional hymn of tribute to Russian patriotic pride, nor was he primarily concerned with the nature of military conflict in itself. There were already enough grand panoramic surveys of battles, marches and retreats: copies of them were in his own library, together with many of the memoirs of the time. Tolstoy's purpose was different. Although he respected self-sacrifice and personal courage, he knew from what he had seen in the Caucasus and the Crimea that war is a senseless tragedy and never a romantic adventure. He was interested, above all, in the dichotomy of human nature, the alternation of selfishness and selflessness both under the stress of dramatic events and within the calmer framework of normal existence. His sense of the past accepted the reality of the historical characters he had encountered in his reading, but his literary imagination sometimes endowed their personalities with tricks of behaviour noticed in others during his days of service: thus the Kutuzov of Tolstoy's novel becomes a simpler and nobler figure than the Kutuzov of history, and some of the lesser officers – particularly in the Grand Army – seem to show the affectations of the Second Empire rather than the First. Yet none of Tolstoy's creative licence is anachronistic: his interpretation is at least as valid as the reminiscences of a participant written years afterwards, when later reflection unconsciously intrudes on the memory, distorting motive and occasionally the chronicle of events as well.

For his non-historical characters Tolstoy looked almost entirely at his own family and the Behrs family, into which he married. Not all of them were known to Tolstoy himself, and his portraits accordingly have at times the slightly exaggerated features of a caricature based on hearsay and legend. The old Prince Bolkonsky, for example, is generally accepted as having been modelled on Tolstoy's maternal grandfather, Prince Nikolai Volkonsky, a veteran of Catherine II's wars who did indeed die in 1812. Many of the prototypes for the aristocrats had themselves lived through the heroic years though none had been so close to the centre of affairs. Tolstoy's mother, Marya, had many of the characteristics of Princess Marya Bolkonska in the book, although the deep religiosity of the fictional Marya seems to have been drawn from one of Tolstoy's aunts, Countess Osten-Sacken. At the time of Napoleon's invasion, Tolstoy's mother was twenty-two years old and his aunt was fifteen. Leo Tolstoy never knew his mother (who died before his second birthday) and only knew Countess Osten-Sacken towards the end of her life, when he was himself still a schoolboy. He heard about the Volkonsky household from a cousin of his mother who visited her uncle, Prince Volkonsky, many times in the Napoleonic period. The principal survivor of those years close to Tolstoy was an old friend of his family, Tatiana Ergolskaya, who became legal guardian to the young Leo on his father's death. She was herself a woman of twenty when

Moscow fell, and she continued to live at Yasnaya Polyana through-out the years in which Tolstoy was engaged in writing *War and Peace*.

It is with the creation of the Rostov family that the Russia of Leo Tolstoy imposes itself most forcibly on the historical background. Count Nikolai Rostov is a composite of two members of Tolstoy's family who had lived through the period covered by the novel, his own father and his paternal grandfather. Similarly Countess Rostova's prototype was Tolstoy's grandmother, aged fifty in 1812. The Rostov daughters, on the other hand, are both based on a markedly different age group: Vera Rostova is modelled on Tolstoy's elder sister-in-law, Elizaveta Behrs; and Natasha is a mixture of Tanya Behrs and (particularly in the domesticated section of the First Epilogue) of Sonya, Tolstoy's wife. We learn from Chapter v of Book 1 that Nata-sha Rostova was born in 1792; but Sonya was only eighteen when Tolstoy married her in 1862 and Tanya was over two years younger. There is thus a gap of nearly three generations between the fictitious Natasha and the two girls on whom she was modelled. Tanya Behrs (or, as she later became, Tanya Kuzminskaya) left memoirs in which she described her 'life at home and at Yasnaya Polyana', and there is no doubt that many incidents in the Natasha story are based on her experiences in the 1860s; thus Tanya maintains that the description of Natasha's feelings at the Grand Ball on New Year's Eve, 1810, rests upon what she told Tolstoy of her own sense of desolation and ultimate delight during her own first ball at Tula in the presence of the young Tsarevich Nicholas, a romantic figure soon to die from consumption. There is, of course, no reason why a young girl's emotions should be different on such an occasion, whether it be in 1810 or 1864. The atmosphere would be the same; the dress uni-forms hardly altered; and, since Russia accepted ballroom waltzing earlier than in the West, there would have been little change in the principal entertainment of the evening. No doubt innocent flirtations were just as changeless, too. Tolstoy's account loses nothing in authenticity through the passage of half a century.

The first part of *War and Peace* was published in a Russian periodical in February 1865, just sixty years after the events it narrates; and the final instalment appeared in November 1869. Tolstoy, however, con-tinued to revise and prune his work for another four years and it was not until 1886 that the standard and definitive edition of the novel was produced. The serialisation of *War and Peace* was well-timed, for the long age of general stability between the Powers, begun in 1815, was at last breaking down. The 1860s were a decade of war: the new Prussia of Bismarck and Moltke was on the march in Europe; the massed formations of Union and Confederacy were locked in battle over an area greater in extent than any ravaged by Napoleon; French regiments were fighting for a new Empire in Mexico; and in Latin America Paraguay began a campaign against her neighbours in which she suffered as many deaths from war and disease as the armies of both antagonists in 1812. Within the Russian Empire the army was in action against Polish rebels and central Asian tribesmen during the sixties and a mood of imperial patriotism began to excite the reading public (such as it was) in the cities. To Tolstoy's intense irritation many Russians, deeply moved by the patriotic passages in *War and Peace*, failed to see that the book was a sustained condemnation of the evils of war and of the folly which induces a disingenuous military commander to believe his own will determines the outcome of a campaign, the issues of so-called victory or defeat. Tolstoy's genius was recognised when *War and Peace* appeared, and so was the original nature of the novel's structure; but his mission remained only partially perceived. Hence the care with which he subsequently revised those sections which touched on moral questions and on the philosophy of history. He was anxious that his masterpiece should be accepted, not only as a work of literature, but as a tract for all times, a sermon on the virtues of the open soul.

The conflict between Tolstoy's realism and his idealism, between what he was and what he thought he believed, intrudes increasingly in his other novels. In 1875 he began his second great work, *Anna Karenina*, which he completed two years later. On this occasion he was more concerned with social tensions within a family than with individuals caught up in the whirlpool of history, and rather than set his narrative in the recent past he chose a contemporary setting. But Tolstoy's Russia was by now changing: if *War and Peace* was lit by the flames of Holy Moscow, then *Anna Karenina* was lit, from first chapter to last, by the roaring flames of an express train thundering across the immense space of Russia. And though Pierre in the one novel and Levin in the other have so much in common that they might well have been born in the same year, the differences between them reflect successive phases in Tolstoy's reaction to his Russia. Pierre, created in the era of Alexander II's reforms, hopefully seeks the unattainable; but Levin, created when repression had returned to Russian society, restlessly despises material comforts unless he can find some key to the riddle of life itself. So it was to be for Tolstoy himself. At the age of fifty he rejected his old beliefs and habits; he sought spiritual elevation by honouring peasant simplicity; and as an ethical teacher he felt himself to be reborn.

For most of the last thirty years of his life, Tolstoy stood aside from the mainstream of Russian development, although the miseries of the famine in 1891 led him to spend the winter organising food kitchens in Tula Province. His social anarchism was a severe strain on his wife and on the happiness of their marriage while, at the same time, tending to isolate him from the affairs of the world. The energy with which he propagated his views won him disciples in other parts of Russia as well as in Sweden, Britain, Holland and the United States. Not all 'Tolstoyans' were honest while others had genuine difficulty

in understanding the master's ideas; but many somehow made the journey to Yasnaya Polyana in the closing decades of the old century and at the opening of the new. Their presence at Yasnaya destroyed the 'Bald Hills' atmosphere which Tolstoy had captured in *War and Peace*. 'It is strange to see Tolstoy among the Tolstoyans,' wrote Maxim Gorky, 'There stands a majestic belfry whose bell resounds ceaselessly all over the world; and around and around scurry cautious little curs who yap to the tune of the bell, stealthily, suspiciously eyeing one another to see which will yap the best.' Just as Ruskin denied being a Ruskinian and Karl Marx being a Marxist, so Tolstoy insisted he was no Tolstoyan; and at times there is no doubt that these proto-hippies mightily taxed his limited resources of patience.

His books continued to arouse both admiration and wrath: 'Such a wonderful, wonderful writer,' sighed Tsar Alexander III, graciously according Countess Tolstoy an audience after the Holy Synod had insisted on banning her husband's *Kreutzer Sonata*. The Tsar hoped –

Above Photograph of Tolstoy in his old age walking in the fields of Yasnaya Polyana. In the background are village huts belonging to peasants on his estate.

Right In the final stage of his life Tolstoy determined to rid himself of worldly entanglements and live in the simple manner of a 'starets'. This photograph of him was taken en route for Yasnaya Polyana from Moscow.

and so did the unfortunate Sonya – that he would at last find inspiration for another *War and Peace*. But what epic was there in Russian life which could fire his creative furnace?

Alexander III died in 1894 and his weak, ineffectual son, Nicholas II, was crowned in Moscow with hierarchic pomp and splendour. Gloomily Tolstoy watched the growing violence in the country. In 1904 reckless imperialism precipitated a disastrous war with Japan, and the old veteran of Sebastopol used the powers that had praised Kutuzov to denounce Nicholas II and his generals for wasting Russian lives in a meaningless campaign. Worse was to follow. In 1905 it seemed as if the Revolution had come at last, and Tolstoy was saddened both by police repression and by terrorist assassinations. The tragedy of his country and the tragedy of his own domestic misunderstandings weighed heavily on his spirits. At the end of October 1910, he fled from Yasnaya, stumbling blindly like Pierre towards the unattainable. He collapsed at the small railway station of Astopovo, and died in the station-master's house seven days later. He was buried without religious rites on a small wooded knoll near Yasnaya Polyana. The Russian people went into mourning.

Select Bibliography

This list of books is in no sense a comprehensive bibliography. It is intended to provide suggestions for further reading in English and to indicate some of the works which I have read with profit while writing this present book and to which I would like to express my indebtedness. To these titles should be added some selections from contemporary sources published in Russian periodicals and historical anthologies as well as three books in French:

Andolenko, S., *Histoire de l'Armée Russe* (Paris 1967).

de Grunwald, C., *La Campagne de Russie, 1812* (Paris 1963).

Vandal, A., *Napoléon et Alexandre I* (Paris 1897).

CONTEMPORARY WORKS

MODERN ANTHOLOGIES

Brett-James, A., *1812, Napoleon's Defeat in Russia* (London 1966).

Cross, A., *Russia under Western Eyes, 1517–1825* (London 1971).

Putnam, P., *Seven Britons in Imperial Russia, 1698–1812* (Princeton 1952).

ORIGINAL SOURCES

Carr, J., *A Northern Summer, Travels . . . in 1804* (London 1805).

Clarke, E. D., *Travels in Various Countries of Europe* (Cambridge 1810), Part I.

James, J. T., *Journal of a Tour in Germany, Sweden, Russia and Poland during the years 1813 and 1814* (London 1817–19), 2 vols.

Johnston, R., *Travels Through Part of the Russian Empire* (London 1815).

Lyall, R., *The Character of the Russians and a Detailed History of Moscow* (London 1823).

Ker Porter, R., *Travelling Sketches in Russia and Sweden* (London 1809–13).

Wilmot, Martha and Catherine, *The Russian Journals*, ed. the Marchioness of Londonderry and H. M. Hyde (London 1934).

Wilson, R. T., *Private Diary . . . 1812, 1813, 1814* (London 1860).

Narrative of Events during . . . 1812 (London 1860).

General Wilson's Journal, ed. A. Brett-James (London 1964).

GENERAL HISTORICAL WORKS

Almedingen, E. M., *Emperor Alexander I* (London 1964).

The Romanovs (London 1966).

Blackwell, W. L., *The Beginnings of Russian Industrialization, 1800–1860* (Princeton 1968).

Blum, Jerome, *Lord and Peasant in Russia* (Princeton 1961).

Cowles, Virginia, *The Romanovs* (London 1971).

Esposito, V. F. and Elting, J. R., *Military History and Atlas of the Napoleonic Wars* (London 1964).

Grey, Ian, *Catherine the Great* (London 1961).

Grimsted, P. K., *The Foreign Ministers of Alexander I* (Berkeley, California 1969).

Jenkins, Michael, *Arakcheev, Grand Vizier of the Russian Empire* (London 1969).

Kochan, M., *Life in Russia under Catherine the Great* (London 1969).

Lefebvre, G., *Napoleon*, (London 1969), 2 vols.

Markham, Felix, *Napoleon* (London 1963).

Palmer, Alan, *Napoleon in Russia* (London 1967).
   Metternich (London 1972).

Pares, Bernard, *A History of Russia*, Rev. ed. (London 1953).

Riha, Thomas, *Readings in Russian Civilization—The Decembrists* (Chicago 1964).

Seton-Watson, Hugh, *The Russian Empire, 1801–1917* (Oxford 1967).

SOME BOOKS ABOUT TOLSTOY

Asquith, C., *Married to Tolstoy* (London 1960).

Behrs-Kuzminskaya, T., *Tolstoy as I Knew Him*, Rev. ed. (New York 1948).

Berlin, Isaiah, *The Hedgehog and the Fox* (London 1957).

Christian, R. F., *Tolstoy's War and Peace* (Oxford 1962).

Gorky, Maxim, *Reminiscences of Tolstoy, Chekhov and Andreev* (London 1948).

Maude, Aylmer, *Life of Tolstoy*, Rev. ed. (Oxford 1930), 2 vols.

The quotations on pages 58–9 and 142 are from L. and A. Maude's translation of *War and Peace* (Macmillan & Co. Ltd. and Oxford University Press, 1942). Those on pages 63, 64, 67, 69, 74 and 97 are from the *Russian Journals of M. and C. Wilmot* edited by Lady Londonderry and H. M. Hyde (Macmillan 1934).

Acknowledgments

The author and publishers wish to record their gratitude for permission received from owners, agents and photographers to reproduce the following list of illustrations (numbers refer to pages):

BLACK AND WHITE ILLUSTRATIONS
Photo Bulloz 144, 160–1, 170–1, 191
Françoise Foliot 89 left and right, 111
Photographie Giraudon 39, 166, 186, 194
Heeresgeschichtliches Museum, Vienna 108
Historisches Museum der Stadt Wien 36
Victor Kennett 29, 41, 66, 73, 74, 82, 84, 85 right, 102, 118
Kunsthistorisches Museum, Vienna 147, 148
The Mansell Collection 52, 54, 81, 92, 95, 128 right, 138, 193, 194 right
Mary Evans Picture Library 57
Nationalmuseum, Stockholm 35
Novosti Press Agency 17, 19 above and below, 21, 27 above, 28, 30, 40, 49, 51, 53 above, 62 above, 64, 71, 75, 84, 101 bottom, 120 below, 135, 137, 152, 155, 159 above and below, 160–1, 177, 183, 185, 207, 209, 216
Radio Times Hulton Picture Library 13, 27 below, 58, 59, 61, 76, 87, 90, 101 above, 112, 113, 117, 120 above, 121 above and right, 124, 128 below left and right, 141, 164, 178, 201 right
Society for Cultural Relations with the USSR endpaper, 43 (and John Freeman) 55, 165, 167, 168, 199, 203, 207, 208, 212
Victoria and Albert Museum, London 188
Roger Viollet 23, 25, 67, 79, 89 below, 104, 156, 172, 176, 181, 195, 202

COLOUR ILLUSTRATIONS
Apsley House (photo Sally Chappell) 80
Photo Bulloz 65
Françoise Foliot 14, 162, 175 above
Victor Kennett 3, 68 below and above, 77, 175 below
Louvre (photo Scala) 114–5
Novosti Press Agency 2, 15
Radio Times Hulton Picture Library 163
Palais de Versailles (photo Bulloz) 126–7
Victoria and Albert Museum (photo John Freeman) 174

Index